stemx

DIVERSITY, EQUITY & INCLUSION
AT THE *SPEED OF THOUGHT*

stemx

DIVERSITY, EQUITY & INCLUSION AT THE *SPEED OF THOUGHT*

MALCOLM ALLEN

Forbes | Books

Published by Forbes Books, Charleston, South Carolina.
Member of Advantage Media.

Forbes Books is a registered trademark, and the Forbes Books colophon is a trademark of Forbes Media, LLC.

Printed in the United States of America.

10 9 8 7 6 5 4 3 2 1

ISBN: 978-1-955884-35-8 (Hardcover)
ISBN: 978-1-955884-61-7 (eBook)

LCCN: 2022915066

Cover design by Analisa Smith.
Layout design by Amanda Haskin.

This custom publication is intended to provide accurate information and the opinions of the author in regard to the subject matter covered. It is sold with the understanding that the publisher, Forbes Books, is not engaged in rendering legal, financial, or professional services of any kind. If legal advice or other expert assistance is required, the reader is advised to seek the services of a competent professional.

Since 1917, Forbes has remained steadfast in its mission to serve as the defining voice of entrepreneurial capitalism. Forbes Books, launched in 2016 through a partnership with Advantage Media, furthers that aim by helping business and thought leaders bring their stories, passion, and knowledge to the forefront in custom books. Opinions expressed by Forbes Books authors are their own. To be considered for publication, please visit **books.Forbes.com**.

CONTENTS

INTRODUCTION

As a young boy, I often dreamed of flying into the light. Sometimes I would sit at my desk and make intricate folds in a sheet of paper, gradually forming it into what I hoped would be "the world's fastest paper airplane."

I experimented with the wings, gauged the width of the body, and studied how each change affected the plane's flight. I wanted an airplane that would fly me away from the murky shores of Lake Providence, Louisiana.

I was born and raised in the America of the 1970s and 1980s, an era of advancement, coupled with stagnation and disappointment. Women's rights increased, the Vietnam War ended, and the world seemed brighter for People of Color. Yet, even as the nation adopted legislation on the heels and hard work of the civil rights movement, those benefits seemed to be fading away.

Nonetheless, African Americans had made some progress. People of Color were achieving gains in education and economic status that their parents had never thought possible. More Black people owned homes, more graduated from high school and college, and Black workers made more money—not a lot more, but the difference seemed to indicate a degree of permanent progress.

That wasn't true in Lake Providence. We were famous for our poverty. In 1994, *Time* magazine ran a story under the headline "The Poorest Place in America." I'd managed to get out by then, but it was a narrow escape. Like every other kid there, I'd wanted to break free, but none of us knew how. We were isolated on an island of poverty in a forgotten sea. None of us had any idea what lay beyond our limited horizons.

My family was lucky enough to avoid our community's worst poverty. By the standards of Lake Providence, we did well. We weren't even close to rich, or even "comfortable," but my dad had a job that paid reasonable wages, we had a roof over our heads, and we could always put food on the table. Our house should've been a welcome refuge from the outside world, but the town's darkness pervaded every room. That darkness sucked all the joy from a young man's life and promised only sadness.

I'm not sure if it was a calling or a mission or the sensation of loft under my wings, but like many boys, rich and poor, those paper airplanes introduced me to the science of aerodynamics, the technology and engineering of design, and the mathematics of geometrical proportion.

I didn't know it at the time, but this was my opening to the world of STEM.

Looking back on it, those tasks might have been easier with a few friends. One of us might have been better at wings, while another could have concentrated on the plane's body. Someone else might have figured out what grade of paper worked best. Maybe I could have taken on management of the project, making sure we all worked toward the same vision, each team member using his or her talents effectively.

If that had happened, it would have been my introduction to diversity as well. But it didn't happen. Lake Providence wasn't the kind of place where people pulled together in a spirit of cooperation. Like everyone everywhere, we gathered in schools, churches, and commercial establishments, but this never produced much community spirit. That had been lost to poverty and ignorance.

Another obstacle to diversity lay in the town's demographics. Nearly all the kids I knew had similar backgrounds: local, Black, and poor. Still, if we had cooperated to build something, diversity would have positively impacted the results. Even when people are of the same race and come from the same town, each person has his or her own individual talents. When you put two different people together, new viewpoints emerge.

My dad once said, "It's not about where you are from; it's about where you are going." That helped me understand my biggest problem: how to free myself from my childhood home.

In Lake Providence I was growing into a man's body, but I had no clear idea of what that meant. Role models were in short supply. I didn't know any movers, shakers, or leaders. The preachers and teachers of Lake Providence hadn't inspired me. I wanted to grow up, be a man, and change the world, but I wasn't even sure what that world was or how it might work. Aside from brief glimpses of Memphis, I'd never seen it.

Crime, ignorance, prostitution, and disease were my town's daily facts of life. The only social justice I ever saw was in the impersonal processes of crime and punishment. This wasn't really justice at all, much less social justice. It seemed like a straight line for many young men, with stops to be handcuffed, transported to a courtroom, and then assigned to a prison cell. Most of the men who went down this path never really left it. This made Lake Providence into a place where depression wasn't a mental state; it was a reasonable response to the world around us.

This is what happens in the claustrophobic environment of such an isolated town. Children grow up ignorant, with parents too worn out to care. These communities aren't really alive, but they can't quite die either. As the community fails, hope, knowledge, and justice fail with it.

One thing that might return the gift of hope to towns like Lake Providence would be an inclusive STEM effort bringing everyone in the community together. This program would need to reach beyond the town's borders and add more diverse elements and backgrounds. If an impoverished town was able to join with wealthier white communities, together they could theoretically create teams from a wider variety of backgrounds. But ideas like that never got much traction in Lake Providence.

As a teenager, I knew there had to be something better. When I learned about military options, I immediately investigated them. This led me to go into the navy. There I learned about planes, ships, and rockets and what makes them run. It was my first real opportunity to see the world, and what followed more than lived up to that promise.

Once I was free of Lake Providence, I began to fulfill my potential both as a man and as a professional. The navy took what little STEM knowledge I had, added to it, refined it, and trained me to use it. That education and training has been a benefit throughout my adult life.

This was true even when I revisited Lake Providence. When I finally returned to my hometown years later, I had learned enough to recognize the problems, and I had enough training to begin the process of solving some of them.

In the pages that follow, we explore how STEM disciplines fit into our lives and communities. At the same time, we discover why STEM programs work better when they are diverse, inclusive, and accessible and when they encourage equity. We will meet many of the people who make STEM programs possible and learn what their experiences have taught them.

In this book, we concentrate on the importance of diversity, inclusion, equity, and access in STEM education and training. We look at classrooms, like the ones I attended, and see how STEM programs can transform them. We learn about minority scientists and technicians, women who've bucked the odds to become engineers, and Black mathematicians. These are people who have survived assaults and changed the world. Together, their stories demonstrate the promise of STEM, and our ability to fulfill that promise.

STEM is the hope of the world. I know because as I traveled through Africa, Asia, and Europe, I learned that there are isolated, impoverished communities everywhere. Many of their fundamental problems could be solved through an application of STEM methods and skills.

STEM learning might begin anytime, anywhere. With me, it was the quest for the perfect paper airplane. With another child, it might start with building sandcastles, constructing something from Legos, or peering through the lens of a toy microscope. Wherever STEM learning starts, we need to ensure that it continues. The boy who likes to analyze football statistics should be encouraged, just as we must be ready to help the girl who sees her dollhouse as an engineering problem.

> **STEM is the hope of the world.**

Our modern world is said to hold limitless possibilities, but if we're going to discover those possibilities, we will do it with diverse and inclusive STEM efforts.

STEM is how we got here, and STEM is our only path forward. Diversity is the key to better-quality STEM programs, and with it, we must ensure inclusion, equity, and accessibility.

The choices are clear: we can either ignore STEM disciplines and fall hopelessly behind other countries or embrace diversity in STEM education and training, and step into a better future.

THE MATH OF ROBERT MOSES

On Sunday, July 25, 2021, as this book was in the planning stages, one of America's great civil rights activists, and a pioneer who spread STEM education into Black children's classrooms throughout the world, died at the age of eighty-six.[1] He never sought publicity, and he always told others that he wasn't a leader.

In 1982, when Robert Moses began his Algebra Project at Lanier High School in Jackson, Mississippi, he was already known as a veteran voting-rights organizer. In the early 1960s, he had battled for Black access to the ballot across the American South.

Bob Moses had been born in Harlem in 1935, but he hadn't understood Black influence in American society until he worked in the 1950s as a traveling tutor for the aptly named white doo-wop group Frankie and the Teenagers. The group's members were at an age

---

1   Levenson, Risen, and Medina, "Bob Moses, Crusader."

when they should have been attending school, so they hired Moses to be their tutor whenever they toured. Moses traveled with them, giving lessons, assigning homework, and administering tests.

When they traveled, the laws and taboos of segregation dictated that Moses find lodging in the Black sections of most towns, often in the homes of Black families. This experience showed him the Black urban culture that was emerging in America's cities and towns.

Back in New York, Moses earned advanced degrees and taught algebra in New York City public schools. He did this for three years before traveling through the South, where he dealt with a different kind of math—the numbers surrounding Black voter registration. In Georgia only six out of one hundred legally qualified Black adults were registered to vote. Most of these people wanted to vote, but white officials used every trick, legal and illegal, to stop them.

Moses often had to confront his violent opponents face-to-face. According to his obituary in the *New York Times*, "During a voter-registration drive, a sheriff's cousin bashed Mr. Moses' head with a knife handle. Bleeding, he kept going, staggering up the steps of a courthouse to register a couple of Black farmers." Only then did he seek medical attention.

It turned out that the county didn't have a Black doctor, so law and local custom dictated that Moses "be driven to another town, where nine stitches were sewn into his head." Nine stitches equaled two registered Black voters: that was the kind of equation Bob Moses had to solve during the civil rights movement. It was an unforgiving math with no margin for error.

In 1964 Moses was an instigator and primary orchestrator of Freedom Summer. This event drew hundreds of white and Black students to Mississippi to help register Black folks to vote, in what many considered to be the most violent and racist state in America. In their attempts to stop this effort, a "posse" of white racists in one Mississippi county—including Klan members and men in law enforcement—murdered three of these students, burying their bodies in an earthen dam that was under construction nearby.

Most of the guilty killers escaped justice entirely. A few were convicted and given short sentences for federal civil rights violations. Forty-one years later, in 2005, one perpetrator, Edgar Ray Killen, was convicted on three counts of manslaughter. Although it didn't carry the kind of sentence a first-degree murder conviction would have brought, it was enough to ensure that Killen would die in prison.

Many other civil rights workers, including Moses, were threatened, beaten, shot at, and jailed. Despite these criminal attacks, Moses and his allies prevailed, and in 1965 Congress passed the Voting Rights Act. Just two years after that, in 1967, the percentage of Black adults in Mississippi who were registered to vote had increased from 6% to 57%. Robert Moses could take pride in such a welcome mathematical progression because its real-world consequences were so righteous.[2]

Later Moses traveled to the East African nation of Tanzania, where he spent six years teaching math to children. His work there became the basis of his Algebra Project, which he began developing in the late 1970s. Bob Moses understood the importance of STEM subjects in any worthwhile education, and he knew firsthand the difficulties Blacks faced when learning or training in STEM fields. He once told an interviewer from NPR, "Education is still basically Jim Crow as far as the kids who are in the bottom economic strata of the country. No one knows about them, no one cares about them."

His special gift was in mathematics, so that was what he taught. He knew math literacy brought financial literacy, and with that came more wealth, better health, and a brighter future. "Bob really saw the

---

2   González, "From the Archives."

issue of giving hope to young people through access to mathematics literacy … as a citizenship issue, as critical as the right to vote," said Ben Moynihan, the Project's director of operations.

Robert Moses knew that true equality—the equality that comes with real opportunities to make a better life—can only be achieved with the help of a good education. He recognized that in today's world, the emphasis must be on STEM education. His specialty was mathematics, but he also understood that numbers and mathematical functions are the keys to technology, engineering, and the sciences.

Robert Moses put his life and work on the line so that we might learn the truth. Truth was a goal he shared with other teachers of STEM subjects. This book is dedicated to the late Robert Moses—and to all STEM teachers, living and gone.

CHAPTER 1

URGENT!

A WAKE-UP CALL FOR AMERICAN EDUCATION

Achieving quality STEM (science, technology, engineering, and mathematics) education is a worldwide goal. In every country on the planet, the big question is whether this is achievable and, if so, how. Nations, big and small, are in a global competition to find ways to bring the benefits of quality STEM learning to every child. One of the biggest obstacles to quality is the stagnation that inevitably develops in isolated societies. They may imitate some STEM successes, but ultimately they fail to grow and thrive.

We can see the effects of this competition in the paths of two nations: North Korea and China. North Korea is one of the world's most isolated societies. Its leaders oppose diversity of any kind, eliminating any possibility of inclusion, equity, or access. As they copy foreign technologies, their scientists produce a few threatening missiles and nuclear bombs, but they can't feed or clothe their people.

North Korea's neighbor, China, couldn't be more different. Though China stifles dissent, prior to the COVID outbreak of 2020, they welcomed foreign participation in essential STEM ventures. Even as China locked down to control the virus, the nation's leaders allowed some international projects to continue. When the virus subsides, they have every intention of welcoming more external expertise into their projects again. Though this can lead to the introduction of unwelcome ideas China's leaders want to suppress, they don't want to shut off the flow of imported STEM expertise. As China strives to become the world's biggest, most dynamic economy, they are creating modern education facilities and training programs dedicated to producing the world's best STEM workforce.

China's main competitor is the United States. Of course, China will continue to advance, but that just means America must buckle down, work harder, and use its collective imagination to build the world's best STEM workforce. The US has many of the best scientists, technicians, engineers, and mathematicians on the planet. They are all active participants in America's STEM community. Most of them have some notion of the need for diverse teams that include members from multiple backgrounds, guaranteeing equity and access for all. This should be a global goal. We, who are members of the global STEM community, must shape policies to address that need.

THE STEM COMMUNITY: WHAT IS IT? WHO'S IN IT?

STEM has always been with us. The first human who figured out the workings of a wheel was using it, as was the first to build a hut or sow a field with seeds. In Genesis in the Bible, Noah needed STEM skills to build the ark, and later the Egyptians depended on them as they raised the pyramids.

Though you may not know it, you the reader are probably a member of the STEM community. This community includes anyone who is interested in learning more about STEM subjects. Though most STEM education efforts target young students, many of the rest of us live in STEM environments and work in STEM fields, often without even knowing it.

When we talk about jobs in STEM areas, our listeners usually imagine the same things anyone would: scientists peering intently into microscopes or telescopes or mixing chemicals in labs. Many people hear the words behind the acronym and immediately say, "That doesn't affect me. I'm never going to be a rocket scientist!" But our future rocket scientists aren't the only ones who need STEM skills. Even though we might not be aware of it, most of us use STEM skills every day. They make modern life possible.

If you have doubts, consider the STEM skills that go into a house. Everyone involved in the building of a house uses materials and methods developed by modern science. First, a team of surveyors and landscapers employ the latest technology to describe and grade the lot. Then an architect designs the house in accordance with the latest ideas in engineering. These plans are carried out with mathematical precision by masons, carpenters, electricians, plumbers, painters, and other STEM professionals. They put up a frame, then floors, walls, and a roof, followed by pipes, wires, communication connections, and all the other features that accompany modern life. Together these combine to create the house you or I will live in.

Another good example of STEM's role in our communities is public sanitation. In cities or suburbs, you hear the sounds every day, as the truck engine roars and the compactor wheezes into action. You might think of those folks on the garbage truck as mere manual laborers, but as they recycle our trash and dispose of our garbage, they are using a variety of STEM skills.

The operators of a public sanitation system must follow scientific principles when choosing from various specially designed truck models, each employing a different set of technologies.

The planners must consult with drivers and loaders (primary workers: the ones who empty cans and dumpsters) to engineer efficient methods and routes, locate dumps and recycling facilities, and tie everything together with mathematically expressed measurements.

All of this is required to create a complete sanitation system. Then the truck drivers and loaders (those primary STEM workers) roll down streets and alleys performing functions that make all our lives much healthier. That's what it takes to operate the system that gets rid of the things we don't want.

Many of the people doing these jobs aren't even aware that they are using their STEM educations. No one used the term "STEM" when they were in school. Nonetheless, they learned enough to do their work competently, building our homes and keeping our neighborhoods clean. Nowadays some of them are taking advanced STEM courses to sharpen their skills. They know that the more they learn about these fields, the better they will do their jobs.

Once people grasp what the *STEM* acronym stands for and consider the skills involved, almost everyone sees the importance of STEM education. Most people also understand the links between these four fields and a little about how they work together. They realize that scientists use technology and engineering to develop new products. These products are often defined in mathematical terms. We see this everywhere, from lists of nutrition content on food items to measurements of screen sizes on windows. Together, all STEM skills serve one purpose: they help us build a better world.

> *Diverse teams bring together a variety of viewpoints, allowing them to explore new ideas more fully.*

A similar principle applies to the people who study and work in STEM occupations. They come from different backgrounds, and each one has specialized training, but when they combine their efforts, they perform much better than they would if each were working alone. That's because diverse teams bring together a variety of viewpoints, allowing them to explore new ideas more fully. In these circumstances, the whole is always greater than the sum of its parts.

THE CURRENT STATE OF DIVERSITY, INCLUSION, EQUITY, AND ACCESS IN STEM EDUCATION

Equity, access, inclusion, and diversity should be basic parts of any STEM education program. Equity guarantees that every student will be given equal opportunities; access provides those students with information; inclusion gets them in the door; and diversity guarantees that, while they might see faces like their own, some people on their team will be very different.

In most cases, this creates an environment where honest expression is welcome and team members respect one another. This is when mentoring becomes a mutual activity that benefits everyone involved. That's why diverse STEM teams usually deliver better results.

STEM education needs to improve in all four of these areas. Too often diversity and equity are remote goals, inclusion is an afterthought, and access is denied. Without these functions there's no opportunity for mentorship. Consider the following statistics:

- A Pew Center report found that Black students made up only 7% of STEM graduates in higher education, barely half of the proportion of Black people in the total population.[3]

- According to the National Center for Education Statistics, only 2.9% of STEM graduates were Black women, and only 3.8% were Latinas.[4]

---

3   Funk and Parker, "Diversity in the STEM Workforce."

4   US Department of Education, "Number and Percentage Distribution."

- After decades of slow but steady progress through the late twentieth century, since 2004 the percentage of Black STEM graduates has been in a gradual but alarming decline.

These numbers should concern anyone who cares about diversity in education. As we are about to see, some of the most concerned people are household names.

BLACK CELEBRITIES WHO KNOW THE VALUE OF STEM

One might assume that the biggest advocates for boosting opportunities in STEM would come from governments, institutions, or even educators themselves. Yet surprisingly, the people gaining the most ground for marginalized communities and People of Color in STEM come fresh off the stage of global celebrity. These famous personalities are using the platform of their fame to help build a more inclusive, equitable, and sustainable future for STEM.

One famous entertainer who wants to do something about it is the front man of the Grammy Award–winning Black Eyed Peas: will.i.am. This rapper-turned-X-Man passionately believes in a hands-on approach to STEM. As Kristen Castillo wrote, will.i.am is "passionate about education. The 'Scream and Shout' singer is specifically committed to STEM education, helping students as young as elementary school age learn science, technology, engineering, and math."[5]

This passion eventually moved will.i.am to create the i.am Angel Foundation. Through this entity, he partnered with the California

---

5   DeAngelis, "Celebrities and STEM Education."

Endowment, and together they established the i.am College Track.[6] This nationwide program encourages underserved kids to attend and complete college, while emphasizing STEM courses and majors.

After starting with sixty young students, the program swelled to five times that size. The current number of three hundred students is deceptive. Hundreds more crowd the waiting list to get in. This excites will.i.am, but he finds even greater inspiration in the accomplishments of the kids who get the chance. "Our kids went from having a .72 GPA to now having a 3.5 to 4.0," he says proudly.

A welcome newcomer to the ranks of celebrity STEM promoters is NBA superstar LeBron James. Through an organization he had already created, the LeBron James Family Foundation, James began working with Akron's public schools to start that city's new I Promise School.[7]

Beginning with at-risk third and fourth graders, the program offers STEM education based on problem-solving skills. Though some parts of this have been curtailed during the pandemic, the school plans to expand its services to full classes for grades one through eight in 2022 (or whenever the pandemic subsides).

According to reporter Max Zahn, it takes forty-three staffers to run this school. This includes teachers of the basic curriculum, an assistant principal, a principal, and four intervention specialists. In addition, the school has a general tutor, a gym teacher, an English as a second language (ESL) teacher, and a music teacher. Classrooms have one teacher, with no more than twenty students, Zahn writes, adding, "The most unique feature of the school may be the most ordinary: it's a traditional public school." The uniqueness of this situation arises out of the participation of James.

---

6   i.am Angel Foundation, "i.am College Track."

7   James, "Our Home. Our Family."

Celebrities usually prefer to back charter schools rather than traditional public schools. They often cite the independence of these schools and freedom to experiment as their chief attraction. Often the experiments include new and different approaches to STEM (or "STEAM" when these efforts include the arts).

Madonna helped fund a charter school in Detroit, and Sean "Diddy" Combs started the Harlem Academy in New York City. Other celebrity-backed schools are private and often very nontraditional, such as the forty-student STEM school Elon Musk launched in an unused SpaceX conference room. It's reported that students at Musk's school "play with flamethrowers" in some of their science classes, though they also follow stringent safety procedures and learn a lot about combustion.

The I Promise School LeBron James is backing in Akron doesn't have any flamethrowers, but it does have a variety of perks to keep students and their parents enthusiastic and on board. Its status as a public school ensures that certain standards are met. STEM teachers are trained and credentialed in their subjects.

Small classes guarantee that each student will get personal attention. There's no tuition. Uniforms are free, as are meals and some local transportation. The families of students are given access to a food pantry so they can cut down on their grocery bills. This often eases difficult financial situations at home, reducing students' distractions.

The school also gives each student a free bicycle, along with a helmet.[8] This was something James wanted because of his own experiences. Though in his day he often biked around without a helmet, bicycle transportation was a vital part of his Akron upbringing. James knew what bikes would mean to hundreds of the city's teenagers. As he told one reporter, "A bicycle, for me, was the only way to get around

---

8   James, "We Are Family."

the city. If I wanted to meet some of my friends, travel across the city, go to school, play basketball—anything—the bicycle was the way I got around."

Another celebrity who's been active in STEM education is thirteen-time Grammy Award–winning singer-songwriter Pharrell Williams. As a music producer, Williams earned an Oscar nomination for his work on *Hidden Figures*, a film that tells the story of Black women scientists at NASA during the Apollo program.[9] These women were the pioneers of STEM diversity in the aerospace industry.

Pharrell's mother, Dr. Carolyn Williams, is a veteran educator, who is also a member of the first generation inspired by NASA's Black women. These women helped all of us see our world in a new and different way, but they were especially inspiring to young Black women thinking of careers in STEM.

Dr. Williams has said that her son's interest in STEM grew from his idea that every child, no matter how poor or disadvantaged, should have the opportunity to see the world. "His initial thought was … to create a computer resource center, and that way, with computers, they will have an opportunity to visit places virtually and learn lots of things about different cultures," Dr. Williams said. "[But then] we realized that going to the kids, going to the centers, going to the schools made it more accessible for the kids. And we were able to touch more kids that way."

In his hometown of Virginia Beach, Pharrell began the nonprofit From One Hand To Another (FOHTA) to spearhead this effort.[10] For ten years FOHTA's efforts in Virginia Beach schools grew, until it was serving more than three hundred young STEM students. In 2020 its plans for expansion were going well, but, as with so many activities,

---

9   Shetterly, "Hidden Figures."

10   S. Gregory, "Pharrell Williams' Latest Project."

COVID brought all of that to a halt. Now as the pandemic seems to be easing, plans that have been on hold are being revived. FOHTA—which has now transformed into the YELLOW foundation (named for Pharrell's special relationship with that color)—will soon bring back summer camps for elementary and middle school students and begin its long-delayed pilot high school camp.

As Chief Operating Officer Stacey Lopez writes on YELLOW's website, "In local schools, Students of Color are below their counterparts in math, reading, and far below in college readiness. That's where YELLOW can step in. We want to *even* the *odds* for those kids, to give them the opportunity to find what they're amazing at. We don't want any student to feel like they're below average. We will uplift and educate them. We will help them foster social capital and locate cultural capital. We will give them a sense of agency to create a positive change in their lives and in the lives of others in their communities. We will empower communities through education."[11]

The program's leaders have been consulting with advisors from NASA and Harvard's Graduate School of Education while designing a YELLOW program representing "educational futurism in action: a holistic curriculum, mastery-based learning, immersive experiences, integrated student support, and an emphasis on career and creative skills and self-efficacy." They want to reach out to every student of every kind. "We need our teachers to be able to reach every kid that they put their eyes on," says Carolyn Williams. "We need kids to walk away feeling inspired."

With her famous son backing her, Dr. Williams started their initial STEM program at Virginia Beach's Bettie F. Williams Elementary School in 2010. This first effort provided after-school STEM tutoring. Their targets were students who were struggling and students

---

11   YELLOW, "Change Starts at Home."

with aptitudes for STEM subjects who wanted to accelerate their learning in those fields. Principal Timothy P. Sullivan says that the after-school project continues to this day and still has visible impact.

The program grew into a summer camp in 2012. This is a five-week session, with a schedule Sullivan describes as "a full-day school day, with transportation, breakfast and lunch, a strong STEM curriculum, field trips to museums and NASA, visits from astronauts, Skyping with world-famous contributors to science, and students presenting amazing projects."

This FOHTA program that started at Bettie F. Williams Elementary is set to continue in the post-COVID world under YELLOW, encouraging students to use a process called "dream mapping" to tap into their creativity. Dream mapping builds a bridge between dream science (as in the Science Channel's *Dream Science Classroom* projects) and the creative process. This process brings about collaboration that infuses artistic creativity into scientific endeavors and moves science into the creative framework of art. Digital art is one of the most fun and useful ways to enter what the digital world calls the "metaverse."

YELLOW's unusual curriculum has more than its share of science. Students learn coding, along with other computer science skills, and the school offers classes in the environment and forensics. Guest speakers have included artists, musicians, doctors, and FBI agents.[12]

One class visited a medical school. "The kids were put in stations, and they got to work with various medical procedures," Dr. Williams told an interviewer. "For me, the most powerful [part] was actually seeing and touching organs." Nor do they neglect entrepreneurship. In one class, students research and pitch products the same way contestants do on *Shark Tank*.

---

12   Amazon, "Amazon Teams Up."

In June 2021, as the world suffered through its second year of COVID, YELLOW launched its "Summer of Innovation." One winning entry came from a fifth grader named Kamryn and showed his concern for the homeless.[13] He called it the "Safety Box."

"COVID-19 has changed the world," Kamryn told an interviewer over Zoom. "The Safety Box helps … the homeless because the homeless can't buy masks and gloves and all that. It has masks, gloves, a custom Safety Box T-shirt, hand sanitizer, and the biggest thing about it is a solar sanitizing machine. With the solar sanitizing machine, you could wash your mask and gloves, and it's solar powered, so all you need is sunlight."

The program Williams founded also offers classes in dance and media technology. Languages include Spanish and the Mandarin dialect of Chinese. Teachers use innovative methods and the newest digital tools. Students eat breakfast and lunch provided by the school, and they have a recess period.

YELLOW is one of many ventures that seek to add the letter *A* to the *STEM* acronym. As we noted earlier, the *A* stands for *art*, making the new acronym *STEAM*. Sometimes they also add an extra *M* (*STEAMM*) that, in this case, represents the overall quality of *motivation*, which is essential to the study of all five subjects.

Throughout the country there are many other programs like the ones described here. The world of celebrity has given STEM education some of its greatest allies. But the rest of us are in this too. In recent decades STEM has become the core of basic education all over the world. That makes it everyone's concern.

One big STEM question is, Who will be next? What nation will lead the world toward a future bright with possibilities? It could be

---

13   YELLOW, "Entrepreneur Advice from Kamryn."

China, Europe, Japan, or several other countries, and America is still in the race.

Our best hope lies in our ability to work together with people who are different from us. Their skin colors, features, faiths, and backgrounds may be different, but living in a democracy that respects this and gives people real choices is our biggest advantage. We must learn to treasure our differences and to use them as a tool for learning new skills and methods.

As we put the global pandemic behind us, we must redouble our efforts to give every child a good working knowledge of STEM. This will be our gift to the future.

CHAPTER 2

DECISIONS!

THE SHOES UNDER THE TABLE

"Scientific innovations do not arise *on their own*," wrote Kenneth Gibbs Jr. in a blog post for *Scientific American*.[14] Published in 2014, this post would soon be regarded as one of the most eloquent pleas for improvements in STEM education. Gibbs went on to explain: "Each [innovation] is brought forth through the hard work and ingenuity of scientists. Therefore, the quality of the scientific research enterprise, and its ability to meet the needs of, and positively impact the lives of individuals, communities, nations, and the world is inextricably linked to the [STEM-trained] individuals involved."

14   Gibbs, "Diversity in STEM."

Gibbs was joining a chorus of voices trying to convince scientists, teachers, researchers, and the public of something that seems virtually self-evident: that diversity is the key to successful teamwork, and that teamwork is the key to success in STEM (or STEAM) fields. That chorus is still singing the same song, and their promotion of STEM continues, with Gibbs at the forefront.

Gibbs emphasizes that "diversity refers to *difference*. As such, diversity is a property of groups, not individuals. Although I am a Black man ... I am not diverse. An individual cannot be diverse, but groups of individuals (e.g., the scientific research workforce) can possess diversity."[15]

THE "MAD SCIENTIST" MYTH

Many of our ideas about scientists and their work begin in our own worlds of make-believe. As children, we see movies and TV shows portraying heroic doctors, resourceful technicians, brilliant (if often unstable) mathematicians, and gifted (though sometimes villainous) scientists. Whether heroic or unscrupulous, these isolated geniuses depart from reality in two ways: virtually all of them are white, and each one works alone. A mad scientist might have a shadowy assistant trudging up from the basement, but once the action starts, the white scientist calls the shots. He could be the one building the monster or the superweapon needed to kill it. Either way, it's almost always "he," not "she."

This stress on white male individuals infects our perceptions, influencing our study of scientific history. As Gibbs writes in his essay,

---

15   Boyer, "From Stem Cells."

"In Western cultures, our narratives about science often focus on the singular, 'brilliant' scientist who makes substantial contributions through their innate genius—e.g., Albert Einstein or Isaac Newton."

In school, most of us learn more about the lives of Galileo, Newton, and Einstein than we learn about their discoveries. We see Galileo's endurance in the face of persecution, Newton's inspiration from the falling apple, and Einstein's absentmindedness, which often led him to forget to wear socks. Our teachers hope that any interest we develop in these personalities will lead us to develop more interest in their scientific breakthroughs, helping us learn about those things.

We all get the stories about Franklin flying his kite and about Morse's first message sent by telegraph, but we get little or nothing about their many predecessors and helpers or the assistance those people provided.

Newton once made a famous attempt at inclusion, saying, "If I have seen further, it is by standing on the shoulders of giants," but his giants—such as Ptolemy, Tycho Brahe, and Nicolaus Copernicus—were all white males like him. Also, he hadn't directly worked with any of them; by the time he read their books, they were all dead.

Nonetheless, Newton did have the good sense to recognize that his best work wasn't entirely his own. Though the white men who had influenced him were long gone, he knew he couldn't have come up with his innovative theories if they hadn't already laid the foundation. In this respect, those men were Newton's "team." Today that same "team" has finally added brilliant Black scientists, such as astrophysicist and planetary scientist Neil deGrasse Tyson and MIT computer scientist and digital activist Dr. Joy Buolamwini.

In his famous blog post, Gibbs correctly contends that "teams, not individuals, conduct most scientific research. Thus, the narrative of the brilliant, individual scientist largely fails us in the modern research enterprise." University of California researcher Marlynn Rollins agrees, writing, "Innovations are not spontaneously created; they come from the ingenuity and intelligence of talented individuals working together to problem-solve and achieve goals—and research has shown that diversity can benefit all of these things."[16]

DIVERSITY: THE ESSENCE OF LIFE

Diversity—few words have been used or abused as much as this one. Its dictionary definition is "the practice or quality of including or involving people from a range of different social and ethnic backgrounds and of different genders, sexual orientations, etc." Diversity brings together a variety of intellects and personalities to focus on particular projects or processes.

There are a variety of diversity programs, each with its fans, but some people see the automatic inclusion of minorities as a threat to individual rights and liberties. These skeptics claim that diversity programs rob leaders of the freedom to choose the best-qualified candidates. When detractors make these claims, they can't cite a shred of evidence that will stand up to scrutiny. Virtually all the data points the other way. A society that treasures diversity is made up of individuals. That doesn't change. Each individual thinks and expresses his or her ideas freely. Each also listens, incorporating the ideas of others into his or her own thoughts. This is the picture of freedom.

The society described above is an ideal. But what about teams in the real world? Kelvin Westbrook—president and CEO of KRW

---

16   Rollins, "Diversity in STEM."

Advisors, a consulting company specializing in telecommunications and the media—doesn't hold back about his opinion. He knows the value of diverse input on any wide-ranging decision, but he also knows the diversity must be real. If these people of different colors have grown up with the same backgrounds, biases, and financial advantages, their varied skin tones don't guarantee diversity. Westbrook tells the story of a colleague who once observed that if there isn't a diversity of shoes around a decision-making table, you probably don't have real diversity.[17]

But do diverse teams get the job done? Let's look at the data. Marlynn Rollins summarizes a study from *Proceedings of the National Academy of Sciences* concluding that diverse teams usually outperform their more homogeneous counterparts.[18] This is true even when the homogeneous group is supposed to have "relatively greater ability" than that of the diverse team.

The study supports claims that "diverse perspectives improve collective understanding and collective problem-solving." Marlynn Rollins is unsurprised at the study's finding that "people with different backgrounds have different experiences and perspectives, and because of this, they approach problems differently, ask different questions, and develop more innovative solutions."

Diversity is a basic principle at work in science, and that includes work in modern biology. Diversity is one of the first requirements of life. We find it even in the simplest cell. Its nucleus is different from its cytoplasm, and both are distinct from the membrane covering them. The first living thing couldn't form until a diverse set of elements and circumstances coalesced and started functioning as a unit. That simple, single-celled microorganism—which we now call a "prokaryote,"

---

17   Furst Group, "Does Your Board Pass."

18   Rollins, "Diversity in STEM."

which didn't even have a membrane or nucleus—employed various methods and materials to survive, find nutrients, and reproduce itself.

Eventually the prokaryotes adapted to new circumstances by bringing in more and more diverse elements. These allowed them to evolve into more complex life-forms and, eventually, into us. Each of us is a unit made up of a multitude of diverse elements; if those elements had remained separate and pure, there would be no life, and we wouldn't be here today.

Diversity is already at work in everything we do; it always has been. It was there when the first man and woman joined to raise a family. It continued playing its part in the lives of their children and grandchildren, its effects multiplying with each passing generation. Eventually our ancestors realized that, just as a family will benefit from the varied abilities of its different members, even greater benefits arise when several distinct families unite into a village or tribe.

If each of those families had possessed the exact same talents and abilities, they would have had far less to gain by uniting with others. Difference creates value whether it's in an animal's body or a community. STEM professionals have proven this countless times. Putting limits on this process of diversification is similar to human attempts to regulate nature; eventually nature wins.

> *Putting limits on ... diversification is similar to human attempts to regulate nature; eventually nature wins.*

Black folks and other minorities are no strangers to STEM fields. Many famous People of Color studied, worked, and still work in STEM-related areas. Bob Moses organized the registration of Black voters in

Mississippi in 1964, and in 1982 he began his Algebra Project in the same state.

Moses started with methods he'd used to teach math to his children. Refining the methods in practice, Moses trained others to use them. This was one of the earliest STEM education efforts in America's Black community. Despite his recent death, the Algebra Project continues to create Black success stories in many countries.

Moses and those who have followed him keep the STEM torch burning, as they bring diversity to classrooms, laboratories, and workplaces. Moses gained fame for his work in STEM. What follows are three stories of people famous for other things, but each has demonstrated a lifelong commitment to his work in STEM.

WILLIAMS, JEONG, AND URSCHEL

Most people old enough to remember Montel Williams may also recognize him as one of the top talk show hosts of the 1990s, but before becoming a TV star, he had graduated from the US Naval Academy with a degree in engineering. He'd used his STEM knowledge through a short but intense navy career. "My focus wasn't as much on building things as it was a way of thinking and a paradigm for problem-solving," he said. "Engineering provides a strong math and science backbone and a framework for analysis. You learn to look at problems by breaking them into their component parts and then putting them back together in a sensible way."[19]

---

19   Kenney, "8 Black Celebrities."

The STEM training Williams received was necessary for the work he did during his pre-TV career in the military. The future celebrity talk show host served with the National Security Agency, collecting and analyzing coded communications. His expertise was a factor in the success of the US invasion of Grenada in 1983. In the years since his talk show ended, Williams, who suffers from multiple sclerosis, has been active in expanding medical options for other victims of the same disease. His STEM education has played an essential role in all these efforts.

Korean American actor-comedian Ken Jeong is familiar to many American viewers for his roles in the movie *Crazy Rich Asians* and the TV show *Community*. Before he became a full-time actor, Jeong was a full-time doctor, and he is still a physician licensed by the state of California. According to a post at nerdist.com, "[Jeong's] medical experience has also come in handy throughout his acting career. On *All About Steve*, Jeong helped the medic on set treat extras who had collapsed from heat exhaustion one day. While on the set of *Hangover Part II* in Thailand, Jeong helped a friend of Ed Helms get treatment for food poisoning over the phone."[20]

Dr. Jeong often speaks at schools, showing how a STEM education might lead anywhere. "Know you're not alone," he recently told an audience. "Everybody has a right to pursue what they want. Whatever reality gives you, you make the most of it and make it your own."

Before joining the Baltimore Ravens, offensive lineman John Urschel was busy racking up a 4.0 GPA while getting a math degree from Pennsylvania State University. Unlike some pro-bound college athletes, Urschel didn't think of his diploma as a mere fallback option. It was during his college years that a professor prodded him to develop his interest in math. Urschel later told an interviewer, "There was

---

20 Trumbore, "Secret Science Nerds."

beauty and rigor to the math that I loved. Beneath the complexity, there was some clarity. The further along I got, I realized that I could find answers to questions that no one had answered before. That was a pretty cool feeling."[21]

Urschel participated in the 2014 NFL draft and was selected by the Ravens. As his pro career progressed, Urschel continued his quest for higher degrees while also teaching math to undergraduates. He played with Baltimore for three years before returning to full-time work in academia.

Sometimes called a "mathlete," Urschel is now studying in a Massachusetts Institute of Technology PhD program. According to his biography in *Forbes*, "Urschel has published six peer-reviewed mathematics papers to date and has three more ready for review. That's a respectable publication history for someone who only started pursuing their PhD at MIT this year. He's won academic awards for his math prowess. All this while playing guard for the Baltimore Ravens."

Williams anchored one of TV's most popular shows. Jeong acts in large casts. Urschel played on a Super Bowl contender. None of these men are strangers to the requirements of teamwork. Williams's TV crew, Jeong's fellow cast members, and the Ravens' football squad are diverse teams famous for their success on TV screens and in stadiums. Williams and Urschel have gone on to join or to create diverse teams in STEM fields.

But STEM and diversity aren't just nice ideas that happen to be current in the world of high achievers. As we've already seen, diversity in STEM is found within all kinds of jobs. While we've noted the roles it plays for the builders of homes and the collectors of garbage, it's also there in the work of a normal, everyday rocket scientist (if there is such a thing).

---

21 Episcopal Academy, "Former NFL Star."

JUST YOUR TYPICAL ROCKET SCIENTIST

Clayton Turner may not be "normal" or "everyday," but he has been putting together diverse teams of exceptional minds for NASA research projects for more than three decades. He began life as an audio recording engineer, helping musicians get the sounds they wanted in various musical genres. After nearly a decade of audio work, he then graduated from the Rochester Institute of Technology. His training and experience earned him a position at NASA, and he's been doing rocket science ever since. In 2019 Turner was appointed Director of NASA's Langley Research Center.[22]

Turner has played key roles in technologies used in Earth observation from space; the space shuttles; the Ares I-X rocket; and the entry, descent, and landing segments of the Mars Science Laboratory. Yet when this consummate rocket scientist was in high school, he failed geometry. Today he looks back and blames it on a lack of "appropriate motivation and energy and drive." He finally tapped into those qualities, and now he finds his challenges on the cutting edge of space technology.

Steve Jurczyk, NASA's associate administrator in Washington, DC, sees two reasons for Turner's success. "First, he has the ability to take complex and challenging problems and break them down and organize them in a way that people working with him and for him could be successful," says Jurczyk. "The second thing is he's just a great team-builder."

Several years ago, when Turner was Langley's chief engineer, he was featured in a YouTube video where he aired his thoughts on

---

22   McDonald, "Clayton P. Turner."

diversity in the workplaces he inhabits.[23] "So, diversity for me is bringing in fresh thought and ideas," he told his interviewer. "The more fresh thought from different perspectives you can bring to a problem, the more solutions you can have.... We have many challenges across the nation, and those are best solved with a diverse set of thought. If we get stuck in one mindset or one set of backgrounds ... we may try to do the same solutions over and over, [while] a new set of ideas may come in for something we've never thought of before. Here at NASA, we see that a lot because we do some of the really challenging things. We take on some of the most challenging problems, and the solutions aren't going to be something you can find in a book.... You need a diverse team bringing in ideas from engineering, business development, education, science, from across the board."

BARRIERS TO BUILDING DIVERSE TEAMS

Diversity and STEM are natural allies but increasing the diversity of STEM teams can be difficult. Our nation's long history of systemic racism joins with sexism and other grim prejudices to produce procedures and systems that favor American-born white males. Often these processes fail to properly consider women and minorities, especially at the entry level. If People of Color can't get in on the ground floor, they won't have a chance to rise.

This frustration makes it unlikely that they will participate at all. They know that a company that minimizes minority hiring at all levels won't allow diversity at the top. This goes back to CEO Kelvin

---

23   NASA, "Clayton Turner—Langley."

Westbrook's story about shoes. If beneath the boardroom table all the shoes are expensive and fashionable, the faces above the table are probably white.

In their paper "Perceived Gender and Racial/Ethnic Barriers to STEM Success," authors Jennifer Grossman and Michelle Porche demonstrate that discrimination has remained a significant barrier for ethnic and other minority students at all levels of education.[24] A summary of their study states, "For minority students, discrimination has negative impacts on grades, value of education, academic curiosity, self-efficacy, academic motivation, and achievement. Students who face discrimination are also more likely to doubt their abilities in math, science, and general academic skills. On the other hand, a more diverse group of peers is linked to more positive academic outcomes. By creating a more inclusive environment, providing education in implicit and explicit bias, and doing more holistic reviews of students and job applicants, greater diversity can be achieved."

These systemic barriers of implicit and explicit bias keep minority newcomers from reaching professional success and often cause problems in their mental and physical health. A long list of studies has consistently shown that the effects of bigotry based on race, ethnicity, and sex can damage mental and physical health, creating a chilling effect on the quality of a student's or worker's daily output. This can happen despite parental support or even teacher interventions.

This makes a kind of grim sense. Racism, bigotry, and sexism are imposed from the top, and so for workers, they often appear to carry legitimate authority. When this abuse of authority is systemic (as it often is when we see it at the top), it infects each action and relationship. Everything suffers, from a student's self-motivation to her final grade.

---

24 Grossman and Porche, "Perceived Gender."

Women and minority students who become pioneers in fields or programs dominated by white males often work under additional pressures, many of them hidden. Students from absent or underrepresented minorities are sometimes hurt by the overblown expectations that go with being "first." Jackie Robinson was a perfect example. The first Black man to break modern baseball's color line had to play at the highest level simply to survive.

Many pioneers are expected to perform to higher standards while dealing with the ignorance of colleagues. Often, they find that their teachers and classmates have little cultural awareness of minority concerns or interests. These trailblazing scholars often find the crowd of white male faces surrounding them to be intimidating. This intimidation increases with each inadvertent slight or intentional slur.

One government organization directly addressing these barriers when hiring STEM professionals is the Federal Deposit Insurance Corporation (FDIC). As Nikita Pearson, director of the FDIC Office of Minority and Women Inclusion, recently put it, "The FDIC can play a bigger role, within our mandate, in addressing inequities. When we help remove obstacles in the banking system that stand in the way of people achieving their very best, we strengthen society as a whole."[25]

In March 2021 the FDIC released a new strategic plan for the promotion of "diversity, equity, and inclusion (DEI) in every aspect of its mission and operations." When introducing the plan, FDIC chair Jelena McWilliams stated, "My goal is to build and maintain an FDIC workforce that is talented, diverse, and committed to fostering a safe, fair, and inclusive workplace and banking system…. We will work toward an inclusive FDIC where all feel that they belong."

The FDIC is not only creating a diverse workforce; it is also doing its part to teach basic financial math to young people and anyone

---

25   FDIC, "Diversity and Inclusion."

who missed out on that education. The FDIC is all about banking, and banking is all about math. That's why one traditional (predigital) STEM skill was balancing a checkbook. This was a key to financial responsibility, and anyone who did it had to be comfortable with basic arithmetic, a cornerstone of mathematics.

One primary tool the FDIC has created to teach financial literacy is the Money Smart program.[26] This program features financial education for citizens of every age and circumstance. The most comprehensive and basic part is the Money Smart for Young People program, which can be used in classes K–12. It's where the checkbook gets balanced, though now the checkbook has shifted into digital form.

There are also separate Money Smart courses for young adults, adults, small businesses, and older citizens. These can help students of all ages and backgrounds master the STEM skills they need to manage their day-to-day lives.

Solutions are as diverse as STEM classrooms should be. Each set of circumstances is different, as are the individuals involved. A 2019 study authored by Aaron Fisher at the University of California, Berkeley, found that when minority and women graduate students were certain about their departments' expectations and felt prepared for the course material, they produced the same number of original papers as their white male counterparts. This shows that confidence, clarity, and academic acceptance can go a long way toward the creation of diversity.

As Marlynn Rollins writes, "Students who face discrimination are more likely to doubt their abilities in math, science, and general academic skills, [but] a more diverse group of peers is linked to more positive academic outcomes. By creating a more inclusive environment, providing education in implicit and explicit bias, and doing

---

26   FDIC, "Resources: Money Smart."

more holistic reviews of students and job applicants, greater diversity can be achieved."[27]

The first element we need to make and to consolidate gains in diversity is equity. We will explore this in our next chapter.

---

27   Rollins, "Diversity in STEM."

CHAPTER 3

FREEDOM!
PATHWAYS TO STEM

The first letter in the *STEM* acronym stands for *science*. Science has proven that students learn a lot more when they are in environments that support diversity. While it's one thing to let students into a school, the real test comes when we challenge the school to support equity. In short, that means a school must give every student equal opportunity to learn and achieve. Without those opportunities, *STEM* is just another acronym.

Too many schools and educators ignore the needs of students from diverse or disadvantaged backgrounds, concentrating most of their efforts on students who arrive from affluent homes with all the traditional advantages. That's the easier route for a variety of reasons.

Students who come from homes where they've had advantages have already learned to express themselves appropriately in an academic setting. Their privileged status gives them a reservoir of background information, so they arrive already familiar with the basic format. The science they study was discovered, developed, and distributed in white-run institutions. It is part of a culture these students have known all their lives.

For centuries, every aspect of Western scientific expression and communication occurred in a white environment. Although this is changing, Students of Color from less affluent circumstances still have a lot more to learn just to get started.

ANGEL'S ROAD TO STEM

This was the situation STEM student Angel D'az faced. Angel was born in El Salvador, but his parents brought him to the United States when he was still a baby. Writing in a blog post, he told readers, "For the first 15 years of my life, most of what I knew was the Salvadoran culture of my parents. I was 12 years old when I first noticed someone spread peanut butter with a butter knife. I thought knives were only for cutting. This type of blameless ignorance has led to struggles and wonder during my budding STEM career."[28]

When Angel reached college, he hadn't yet started any advanced STEM studies, and he didn't think of STEM as the focus of his plans. When he graduated from high school, his dream was to become a musician, so his efforts were in the arts—the *A* we insert when we expand *STEM* into the acronym *STEAM*.

Though his interest in science hadn't yet developed, Angel's ambition to succeed was obvious. From the start, he worked harder

---

28 Kunche, "Meet Angel D'az."

and trained harder. "I spent three years as an obsessed musician, practicing my trombone out of a fear of failure," he wrote later. "I started college in 2010 as a music major. I eventually found Business Analytics as a career path in 2015."

As Angel grew up in his American home, his immigrant parents tried to shelter him as much as possible. Their own childhoods had been marred by the brutal civil war in El Salvador that raged through the 1980s. In the 1990s, they married and had Angel. He was still a tiny child when his family began the dangerous trek to the US. There were four national borders and nearly two thousand miles between them and their goal. They had no car, little money, and only the necessities they could carry. Before they reached America, Angel fell ill and almost died.

As they continued north, their journey became even more traumatic, marred by a kidnapping and increasingly desperate border crossings. Finally, they reached the US. Though a hard life awaited them in America, they had faith in a future where they could enjoy the benefits of their labors in a modern country where peace and freedom ruled.

Angel's story isn't unusual for those People of Color who are new to the United States. Like other immigrants throughout history, these newcomers worked hard and looked forward to the day they could climb out of poverty. Angel's family began their new American life in a studio apartment with five other tenants. Nothing could dampen his parents' spirits. The cramped space and lack of privacy were minor irritants compared to what they'd left behind.

While Angel's mother was pregnant with his little brother, she slept on a mattress salvaged from a nearby dumpster while her husband passed his nights on the floor. "My parents were 'low-skill' immigrants, but extremely 'high-grit,'" Angel writes. "My mother stayed at home until she could work during school hours, and my father was a manual laborer.... He soon became a roofer and, after saving a little capital, started a towing company with my mother. Throughout this, they both went to English night school."

Angel's parents' main motivation for working so hard was their need to create a future for their children. They took advantage of the opportunities they found in America. These immigrants had faith in the road ahead, knowing life would be far more prosperous in the United States than it had been in their home in El Salvador. Angel writes, "Occasionally, my father came home from work and said, '*Miren vichos* [Look boys]. Put your hands next to mine.' He placed his calloused, scarred, and greasy hands on the dining room table. My brother and I placed our small, smooth, brown hands next to his, and he stated, 'You will do better than me.'"

Even in these impoverished circumstances, Angel's family was better off than they would have been in their native country. The best his parents could have expected in El Salvador would have been survival amid grinding poverty. Even if they escaped war, their parents' experiences and their own had led them to expect short, sad lives with little possibility of improvement. In America, Mr. and Mrs. D'az could inspire their children with real hope. They could climb the ladder and make successful lives for themselves and their families.

It was the details that often stopped them. As Angel writes, "My guidance was strong on the big picture but lacking in all the little steps. I did well in elementary school with my mother's encouragement but collapsed under the weight of middle school and high school. My parents were woefully unequipped to teach algebra or provide white-collar career guidance or tutors. They despaired at my endless stream of Cs and Ds in high school. There was no knowledge of SATs, ACTs, college admission processes, etc."

Angel's academic performance finally improved when he reached college. His marks in high school had gone up enough that he could get in the door. Although he took some wrong turns and spent "two years jumping between engineering, marketing, and finance," in the end he earned far more than the minimum number of credits he needed. At graduation, his 3.27 GPA was better than he'd expected.

During most of his college years, Angel lived on his earnings from delivering pizzas. With that money he was also able to pay some of his tuition, lowering his future debt from student loans. When he finally graduated, he'd earned a BS in business and economic analytics with a minor in computer science. He was also just one class short of a minor in applied mathematics. Angel was ready to find his own STEM profession.

Angel's tech career began with the job he had in college. "I started by collecting data from delivering pizzas," he told an interviewer. "It started off as an Excel project, which led to Python, which led to statistics, and even giving a talk about it at PyData 2018. I think the best way to develop skills is to follow your own curiosity. If you have an internal question, you learn so much from the process of answering it yourself."

Angel chose to work in business analytics for pragmatic reasons, one of which was his understanding that the color of his skin could be an obstacle in some other related fields. "Specializing in Data Science had too many barriers to entry for someone like me; a budding career, Person of Color with only a bachelor's degree."

When asked about the problems he'd faced, Angel said recently, "Most of my difficulties have come from a large personal ambition mismatching with potential employers who have wanted me to 'pay my dues.' Fortunately, I am stubborn and have found people who are willing to take a chance on me. But as a Latino, I have had to go through many rejections to make the career moves that I have wanted."

He also recalled one regret: "I wish someone had told me that tech specialization was achievable even with my Music degree. I would have gotten a Computer Science minor, left school three years earlier and hustled my way into a technical role."

Angel has confronted the problems of skin color, culture, and poverty with the same grit and determination he witnessed in his parents when they were raising him.[29] He recognizes the obstacles but, being from a family of newcomers, he firmly believes he has a chance to succeed. This is one of his few advantages as an immigrant. Many minority Americans who are born and raised here grow up knowing that a lot of their fellow citizens regard them as inferiors. This stops some minority students before they start.

The most blatant form of this bigotry is white supremacy. In America's white communities, this is a disease. It has a history of being passed down through generations, and it infects the thoughts and actions of even the most well-meaning white folks. Its damaging effects are felt throughout our society in more ways than I can list here.

DICKO'S UNWAVERING PATH TO CODE

Racism and gender were the primary obstacles boot camp graduate Dicko Sow had to overcome as she traveled her own unique road to a STEM profession. This talented, young Woman of Color graduated from college with a business degree and had no real thought of

---

29 STATtrak, "The Struggles and Wonders."

working in STEM-related fields. "I actually got into tech completely by accident," Dicko said in a recent blog post. "[I was] in the insurance industry, I felt bored. I didn't enjoy going to work.... I didn't feel challenged, and I wasn't getting paid very well either. I knew I was unhappy ... so I decided that I should try to go to grad school. While doing research into grad school programs and studying for the GMAT, I found an article talking about how learning to code was better than getting an MBA. I was intrigued."[30]

Dicko knew there would be challenges, but she was ready. "I saw that it was a high-paying field. There were lots of good job opportunities, and it seemed interesting. So, I tried learning everything I could about it. I started trying to learn how to code, using resources like Codecademy. I was hooked. It was so hard to wrap my head around everything, but I absolutely loved it."

Dicko has felt the effects of racism and sexism. "I've struggled with feelings of inadequacy, as well as feeling like I don't belong," she told one interviewer. "Often being the only woman or the only Black person (or both!) on my team—I have also been the only Black woman in an entire company before!—this has been a constant struggle." When asked how she had dealt with this, she said, "Perseverance. I've never given up."

In the same interview, she went on to say, "I've struggled a lot working in tech with feeling inadequate. It took me a while, but I finally realized that people in my industry that are good at what they do because they've seen a lot of this stuff before, and not necessarily because they are geniuses. They recognize patterns, which helps them with problem-solving.

"I realized I should focus on learning the fundamentals ... asking why, asking good questions (after spending time trying to solve them

---

30   Kunche, "Meet Dicko Sow."

myself), as well as practicing, practicing, practicing. All of this has helped me continue to develop problem-solving skills."

Dicko recognizes one common problem in people who are drawn to STEM subjects: lack of people skills. "Building up people skills has also been very important, contrary to what I had believed prior to getting into tech," she says. "It's important to be able to communicate effectively with bosses, coworkers, clients, etc. When working at my tech consultancy, we would always say that the technical problems were always easier to solve than the people problems."

Dicko has largely avoided or solved those problems, and she credits much of her success to those who have helped her along the way. "Building a support system has definitely been the reason I have gotten as far as I have today," she says. "I've been lucky to have some of the best teammates I could ever ask for. Teammates that were always there for me. They understood me. They believed in me when I didn't believe in myself, and they taught me to stand up for myself."

Angel and Dicko are constantly striving for opportunities to achieve their full potentials. To do so, they need to get the same chances as their white male counterparts—in a word: equity. Their demands for equity echo those made by minorities in past generations.

HISTORICAL DEMANDS FOR EQUITY

Take the case of Shirley Malcom. In 1963 Shirley was a young, talented, Black high school graduate who had received her acceptance letter from the University of Alabama.[31] The school had just admitted

---

31   Wikimedia Foundation, "Shirley M. Malcom."

Black students for the first time a few months earlier, and whites were still actively (and often violently) opposing integration of "their" university. Malcom decided it would be easier simply to leave the South. Harboring hopes of finding a less racist environment elsewhere, she left her home in Birmingham for the first time.

Traveling all the way from the Deep South to the Pacific Northwest, Malcom became one of eight hundred zoology majors at Seattle's University of Washington. She was the only Black student in the department. Her determination to stay there won her an ally. When another Black student saw her doing well in zoology, her success inspired him to change subjects. "He switched out of his major and came over to zoology," she later told a reporter from the Undark website. "Then there were two of us."[32]

After completing a personal academic program that culminated with a doctorate in ecology, Malcom taught biology to high school students. With her training and education, she should have been teaching graduate students or leading research teams, but that didn't deter Malcom. She put her heart into working with these young learners, and it showed in their performance. That immense dedication eventually earned her an offer from a respected science group: the American Association for the Advancement of Science (AAAS).

Throughout her career, Malcom concentrated efforts on the fight to increase Black and minority participation in STEM fields. In the last decades of the twentieth century, her work, along with the labors of others, led to significant gains in equity.

Today, Malcom is a senior advisor to the AAAS CEO, and she directs its SEA Change Initiative. According to the AAAS website, SEA Change "aims to advance institutional transformation in support of diversity, equity, and inclusion, especially in colleges and univer-

---

32 Smart, "After Years of Gains."

sities." It is one of many organizations working to advance STEM diversity.

However, the 2020 Undark article went on to describe a disturbing reversal of this trend. The reporters wrote, "An Undark analysis of nearly four decades of data on bachelor's degrees awarded in the U.S. suggests those hard-won gains for Black representation in the sciences are quietly slipping away.... Culled from reports issued by the National Science Foundation (NSF), the analysis indicates that after decades of increases, the share of STEM-field bachelor's degrees awarded to Black students peaked in the early 2000s and has been falling ever since."

NSF Deputy Assistant Director of Education and Human Resources Sylvia James called these trends "absolutely concerning for me personally, and from the agency perspective." The reporters for Undark wrote, "Some experts pointed to persistent income inequality and the disproportionate lack of access to quality schools among Black and other minority communities ... but several education and legal professionals also pointed to a more straightforward and sobering correlation: the steady downturn in STEM degrees among Black students ... comes in the wake of a large-scale retreat from specific programs and policies that consider race in admissions, recruitment, and retention in higher education."

According to the data uncovered by Undark,

- in 1981 Black students earned 4.1% of all bachelor's degrees in life sciences awarded in the United States;

- in 2004 this had almost doubled to 7.4%; and

- in the next twelve years that number sank to 6.2%.[33]

---

33   Smart.

The predominant view among educators is that this is occurring due to lack of government and institutional support. "Federal agencies, universities, and private foundations have largely abandoned the use of programs that are expressly limited to underrepresented racial or ethnic minorities," according to Undark.

Women account for less than one-quarter of our nation's STEM workforce.

Women like Dicko Sow and Shirley Malcom are still the exceptions. By any measure, women are underrepresented in STEM careers. A Commerce Department study shows that women account for less than one-quarter of our nation's STEM workforce. Even in healthcare, where women have a traditional advantage due to their high numbers in the nursing profession, they hold only 30% of the executive-level jobs.

INEQUALITY BEGINS EARLY

Inequality begins in the early grades, where STEM education still has a strong bias toward boys. Though many girls express interest in learning about STEM subjects, they often face invisible obstacles in the early years. Gender stereotypes and majority-male classes often discourage girls from enrolling in STEM courses.

Nonetheless, there are bright spots. Though STEM teachers are mostly white, a study from the American Research Association (ARA) found in 2012 that 64% of them were women—up from 43% one generation earlier.[34]

In that same study, researchers examined representative national data and found

- Hispanics now make up 6% of STEM teachers, a threefold increase over the percentage twenty-four years earlier;

- the proportion of Asian STEM teachers rose at a similar rate, going from 1% to 3%; and

- Black STEM teachers have gone an entire generation stuck at half of what they should be.

This is good news for Hispanic and Asian teachers, but the trend among Black educators is alarming. When Black students don't see Black STEM teachers in their classrooms, they often miss the connection between themselves and the subjects they're expected to study.

Tuan Nguyen, a research assistant professor in the College of Education at Kansas State University and one of the ARA report's authors, told an interviewer, "The literature suggests that teachers not only support their students' cognitive development and their learning, but also shape their motivations [and] aspirations. The research community recognizes we need to bring more minority STEM teachers into classrooms." Nguyen noted that women STEM teachers are particularly positive influences for girls, citing studies showing increased confidence among these students and improvements in their test performances.

---

34   Nguyen and Redding, "Changes in the Demographics."

ENCOURAGING GIRLS TO STUDY STEM

One philanthropic group that wants a future with more women in STEM healthcare fields is the Abbott Fund. This nonprofit grew out of Abbott Laboratories, a 133-year-old pharmaceutical company, which has most recently pioneered quick and effective COVID testing. The Abbott Fund still mirrors the concerns of its corporate parent by supporting education and research in science, engineering, and technology.

Partnering with Discovery Education, the Abbott Fund started the Future Well Kids program to encourage ten- to thirteen-year-olds to form healthy habits in areas of hygiene, diet, and exercise.[35] The program started out with the simple goal of increasing awareness about health issues and expanded into studies of health, medicine, and human biology—STEM-related subjects.

The content targets girls in middle school, at an age when many of them are losing interest in STEM. A Microsoft-sponsored study showed young girls' interest in STEM increasing at age eleven but fading before they reach fifteen. The program highlights some of the top female leaders in STEM industries. It's an approach that gives these girls current role models and inspires them to want to build a future where they can reach for the stars.

In doing this, the program teaches kids the *why*, as well as the *how*. When children learn *how* to develop habits of personal hygiene, they also learn *why* those habits are important to physical health. This takes them into lessons about anatomy, physiology, microbes, and biology. In their classrooms, kids often get to peer through modern

---

35   Meyer and Daugherty, "Paving the Way."

microscopes and use other tools of the laboratory. The program provides lesson plans and educator guides with details about family resources and options for continued learning.

The Abbott Fund's Future Well Kids program is an example of building equity in STEM education. It takes kids in underserved schools and communities a big step forward in forming STEM knowledge. This helps young minority students compete on a more equal footing with their affluent counterparts. It's a short but targeted step in addressing issues of equity.

Lack of equity in STEM-related opportunities is nothing new. As early as 1995, a White House policy review concluded that family connections, including generational affiliations with schools, provide white students with underlying advantages over their Black and minority counterparts.

Accompanying these connections were "countless scholarship programs" designed to benefit students who already have advantages. Those students were also far more likely to be white. This is still true today, and it's one reason minority students are earning a smaller share of STEM degrees.

HISTORICALLY BLACK COLLEGES AND UNIVERSITIES

Our nation's Historically Black Colleges and Universities (HBCUs) have tried to reverse this trend. In a July 2020 article on the Science & Enterprise (S&E) website, HBCUs were cited for having "bolstered the self-confidence necessary for many scientists who were taught there to endure and thrive in their fields."[36] It quoted Morehouse alumnus and assistant professor of biology Jeffrey Handy as he described how a Black student can get affirmation just from seeing a Black teacher leading a STEM class.

"A Black chemistry professor would more likely believe in the abilities of a young Black student," he says. The article points out that, according to NSF data from 2006, "3 percent of the faculty across all disciplines at non-HBCUs are Black, [while] about 55 percent of faculty at HBCUs are Black."

The S&E website article shows that this connection between HBCU faculty and students is more than superficial. "Howard [University] math professor Abdul-Aziz Yakubu has found weaker connections between faculty and students when he has taught or visited non-HBCUs," the article states, "including where he received his graduate degree—North Carolina State University. Teaching at [Washington, DC, area HBCU] Howard University 'is a little more personal,' said Yakubu, who is from Ghana. 'Students at HBCUs see their professors as mentors,' Yakubu said, and it's a relationship he doesn't see when teaching at historically white schools."

Despite these efforts, HBCUs are still seeing a troubling decline in the number of STEM degrees they award. Willie Pearson, a sociology professor at the Georgia Institute of Technology, called this "quite disturbing."[37] Pearson noted that more Blacks are attending traditionally white schools. According to the NSF, in 1977 over one-third of Black college graduates in science and engineering came from HBCUs, but by 2014 that had sunk to 17%.

As options have increased, fewer and fewer Black students have chosen HBCUs. This is especially true of students in STEM fields. It

---

36   Alan, "HBCUs Still Putting Blacks."

37   Alan.

is also true that the proportion of Black people who get STEM degrees peaked in the last generation, and now their numbers are stuck in a slow decline. America's HBCU leaders see this problem, and they are looking for ways to solve it.

The reasons for the decline in minority STEM degrees are many. They include the loss of most affirmative action programs, a lack of promotion (producing a lack of awareness) for STEM curricula, and traditional weeding-out methods that target (inadvertently or on purpose) those whose early schooling forces them to play catch-up in their first year of higher education.

HOW HBCUs HAPPENED

The US Department of Agriculture's website gives us some of the history behind the establishment of HBCUs. They began in the late nineteenth century, as whites grudgingly admitted a need to educate Black folks. The idea was to put all the emphasis in Black higher education on agriculture.[38] At that time, most Americans still lived and worked on farms. This was particularly true of Black people, most of whom still lived in the rural South where they'd recently been enslaved.

This agricultural emphasis could be defended as practical, but it also encouraged Black students to remain in farming, rather than moving to cities where they could compete with whites for urban jobs.

Some of these early HBCUs were small two-year colleges, while others were four-year programs that would eventually grow into universities. Many offered balanced programs, including arts and human-

---

38 Peppers, "Celebrating the Agricultural Impacts."

ities. Another silver lining: practical applications of agriculture. Soil is a science, and farming involves technology and engineering, while all farm measurements and accounting are done with math. As farming became a more competitive business, a good farmer needed as much education as any business executive—perhaps more.

An educated Black farmer could usually do as well or better than his white counterparts, but as mechanization increased, fewer farmers were necessary. Black farmers had less land, less credit, and less margin for error, so they were often the first to go.

As the number of American farmers declined, HBCUs broadened their focus, but farming still had a place. According to the US Department of Agriculture (USDA) site, HBCUs now have the task of "ensuring public access to agricultural education, research, and outreach programs [is] equitably distributed to all Americans."[39] The government's efforts in this area remained mired in racism for most of the century following the Civil War, but eventually programs were designed to provide access for everyone.

Today the USDA still works with our nation's HBCUs. The hbcutoday.net website lists STEM programs at thirty-seven of these schools.[40] Many of the combined efforts of HBCUs and the USDA provide access to learning and training for farmers, students, and other stakeholders.

For instance, US lamb and goat production is just beginning to emerge as a growth industry. Delaware State University's Tony Allen has seen the evidence of this at his university on the Delmarva Peninsula, where grazing livestock thrive.[41] According to the USDA

---

39   Peppers.

40   HBCU Today, "HBCUs with STEM Programs."

41   Delaware State University, "Tony Allen Ph.D.: President."

website, "Delaware State University provided [STEM] training and education for farmers who raise nearly 500 sheep and goats."[42]

The story went on to note that 71% of the farmers agreed to alter their practices due to this training. The aim is to create and manage more successful, sustainable sheep and goat farms. Farmers who use these STEM-based practices give themselves a better opportunity to take advantage of the growing market for these meats.

Another HBCU is Alabama A&M University in Huntsville. Their demand for STEM courses is growing at twice the rate of that for courses in other areas. Working with the USDA, the university's teachers have developed "a 4-H program to improve STEM skills among urban youths. Of the youths who participated, 84% demonstrated enhanced critical thinking, problem solving, collaboration, and creativity. Over 1,000 youths expressed interest in STEM careers after participating in the program."[43]

Baltimore's Morgan State University (MSU) is one of the nation's oldest Black institutions of higher learning and is among the leaders of awarding bachelor's degrees to minorities. This venerable HBCU reaches out to minority youth interested in studying STEM fields through several programs. Morgan is good at finding high-profile partners, including the National Aeronautics and Space Administration, or, as it's commonly known, NASA. Their program helps bridge the gap between K–12 education and college, developing interest and retention in STEM learning through elementary, middle, and high school.[44]

The MSU-NASA collaboration includes a summer program in Actuarial and Mathematical Sciences for rising high school seniors and incoming college freshmen. It's free and lasts for six weeks. Students

---

42   Peppers, "Celebrating the Agricultural Impacts."

43   Peppers.

44   Wilson, "Baltimore SEMAA."

who take the program are offered instruction in precalculus. They also go on field trips and perform studies. Finally, they get coaching in professional development—an area where minority students often need help with access.

DELAWARE STATE UNIVERSITY DEFIES THE ODDS

One HBCU leader who believes that this trend can and should be reversed was mentioned earlier, Delaware State University president Tony Allen. Allen was appointed to the presidency of DSU (an HBCU land grant school established in 1912 on the then-customary agricultural model) after a successful career in banking and public policy. At Delaware, he's raised the university's profile, along with $40 million. When his friend, former boss, and fellow Delawarean Joe Biden was elected president, he named Allen to chair his advisory panel on the federal government's role in supporting HBCUs.[45]

This was no surprise. Tony Allen had started as Joe Biden's speechwriter when Allen was a fresh face from academia and Biden was still in the Senate. Although Tony would earn his doctorate in urban affairs and public policy, he chose to work in communications within the financial sector. That phase of his career began with a job as executive vice president of MBNA America. In 2017 he changed course and dedicated his labors to education at DSU.

Delaware's senator Chris Coons has called Tony Allen "a remarkable leader and champion for HBCUs. As president of Delaware State University, he has helped transform the university into a premier

---

45   Tabeling, "Biden Taps."

center for learning and cutting-edge research that graduates top talent to lead our communities and boardrooms. Dr. Allen has the vision and dedication to continue to advance the vital role that our nation's HBCUs play in serving future generations of American students."

When questioned, Allen puts forth a clear vision of the goal, saying, "I continue to get asked if HBCUs still have relevancy, and my response has always been, 'If you didn't have HBCUs like Delaware State, you'd have to invent us.' There are very few places that can give a four-year comprehensive education … but specifically focus on those often overlooked and underserved."

Tony Allen took the reins at DSU at a moment of profound transition for our entire society. It was January 2020, and there was talk of a pandemic on the horizon. Even to those who were paying attention, this potential disaster seemed distant, but in the following months as the virus spread, Allen adapted, successfully guiding his institution through a worldwide cataclysm.

According to the White House website's profile, "[Allen] and his team have built a strong portfolio of accomplishments focused on student success. The university has seen its elevation to the #3 public HBCU in America (*US News*), an R2 'high research activity' designation, and the historic acquisition of nearby Wesley College. The university's 'Together' COVID-19 plan has been touted as a national example of campus safety strategy, and one year into the pandemic enrollment has shattered all previous records."[46]

---

46   White House, "President Biden Announces."

HBCUs AND THE LIVES OF BLACK SCHOLARS

HBCUs have survived and thrived for well over a century, proving their value from one generation to the next. So, it was a celebratory moment when President George W. Bush appointed Houston school superintendent Rod Paige as secretary of education in 2001.[47] In the early 1950s, Paige graduated from what was then named Jackson College for Negro Teachers in Mississippi. The name reflected the segregation that ruled our nation's higher learning in that era.

In 1967, after the end of legally enforced segregation, the school was renamed Jackson State College. By that time, Rod Paige had returned to coach Jackson's football team to winning records. By 1974, when Jackson State became a university, Paige had departed, taking the helm of the football program at another HBCU, Texas Southern University (TSU). He won there too.

Paige also taught courses, and he was appointed TSU's Dean of the College of Education in 1984. He served in that post until 1994, then began an innovative seven-year term as Houston's school superintendent. The programs he started became the model for the second Bush administration's No Child Left Behind (NCLB) Act.[48] Acting

HBCUs have survived and thrived for well over a century, proving their value from one generation to the next.

---

47   US Department of Education, "Rod Paige."

48   Genatossio, "Roderick Raynor Paige."

as education secretary, Paige helped pass NCLB and implement its provisions.

Paige left the Education Department in 2004, but his connection with HBCUs continued. In 2016, at the age of eighty-three, he was appointed interim president of his alma mater, now called Jackson State University, and served until the following year. Since then, Paige has been a commentator on education issues.

Paige's career shows how HBCUs shaped the lives of generations of Black scholars. When white institutions were closed to Blacks, these schools kept the light of knowledge burning for millions of young people.

EDUCATION IS A CIVIL RIGHT

As Bob Moses always said, in the end, education is our civil right, and we must go after it the same way we pursued voting in the 1960s. "We're using math as the organizing tool, just like voting was the organizing tool," he told one audience two years before his death. "So, math is the organizing tool for us to get the kids to demand their education … but the central strategy that we're using is the same." Moses died believing that education is worth fighting for, and he knew that in today's world, quality education means an emphasis on STEM subjects.

Our policies and programs must change to meet the needs of a modern, diverse workforce. We need to promote equity, rather than letting it drain away. This must be reflected in our thoughts, words, and actions. That's something we all must work on, but in the meantime, students and educators are obliged to do what they can on their own. Aspiring STEM Students of Color should redouble their commitment to excellence. Teachers should do all they can to help these students open new doors.

Angel D'az describes a useful first principle for young minorities in STEM, or any other difficult endeavor. He says, "A lot of us first-gen People of Color have gone through much suffering. It is important we take care of ourselves. We need healthy first-generation People of Color in the tech community."

Persistence, idealism, and health—these are three of the keys we can use to fight for equity in STEM education. Administrators, teachers, and students must train themselves in the application of these tools so that all people have equal opportunities in STEM fields—and once they have equity, they need access, which is the subject of our next chapter.

CHAPTER 4

LET ME IN!
OPENING THAT DOOR

Even in our twenty-first-century world of modern scientific miracles, STEM is the biggest thing going, and the companies operating in STEM fields know it. These companies need access to a steady stream of talent in these fields, so they must encourage STEM education efforts as early as possible in our children's schooling. Students in early grades need to be challenged with science and math problems and taught how to solve them. This is just as true for minority students who traditionally have been left behind in STEM areas.

Access is also the first thing. *All* young people and their parents must find out which schools and teachers fit their needs best, and then they must chart a clear path forward. Teachers need access to the most advanced tools for STEM education. Schools need access to classroom resources and well-equipped laboratories.

Students and teachers can use these features to bring about real learning. Some access won't happen unless there's more funding, but that's not always true. We can create access by streamlining systems, redesigning methods, and, last but not least, opening minds. This last item doesn't have a price tag.

Teachers will lead the way. When a teacher creates an accessible atmosphere that encourages all students to help each other learn together, this gives students access to better education. We can achieve increased access for all disadvantaged students by bringing them to the knowledge or by bringing the knowledge to them. Either approach can work.

Most STEM programs rely on aspects of classroom experience overlapping with real-world topics that are closer to home. For instance, at Boys and Girls Haven, a residential school in Louisville for at-risk children, students went on a field trip to a science center and visited several local companies.[49] The STEM professionals working in those places showed students what STEM careers look like in action.

What's in it for a corporation? Opening access improves its brand in underserved communities, gaining goodwill and giving positive reinforcement of a company's image. One day the company may hire some of the talented students that have benefited from STEM programs the company supported. This helps the company's brand shine brightly, placing it high above the competition. It also creates a positive image in the minds of potential customers.

As American educators increase their efforts to improve diversity in the STEM classroom, the biggest question is whether those efforts will work. Along with that question are the issues of what we are

---

49   Boys & Girls Haven, "A Home & A Future."

measuring and how we measure it. What is our yardstick for quantifying our nation's STEM success? What are the markers for progress, and what is the timeline for reaching them? Overall success should include a growing diversity of talent, a more inclusive environment aimed at accomplishing STEM goals, and better collaboration between organizations and across all sectors in the achievement of those goals.

Educators need accurate measurements to evaluate their students' progress. Corporations need accurate measurements of STEM talents and skills. Using those numbers, they can plan better, design better, and create better products and services for the rest of us.

COMPANIES ENCOURAGING ACCESS

Which companies focus on access to STEM education? There are far too many to mention each one individually, but in the following section are a few prominent examples of companies encouraging access.

Everyone knows Amazon. With a market capitalization of nearly $2 trillion, it's one of the world's largest and best-known companies. We see it every day on our phones and desktops and in the Amazon boxes arriving at our doors. It sells us televisions and provides TV content through Prime in the form of movies and shows. Amazon is a marketplace for entrepreneurs and their products and a publishing platform for writers in every field. There you can find everything from medical supplies to antique model cars. And, of course, you can still buy a book there.

Amazon started as the dream of Jeff Bezos. As a young entrepreneur at the dawn of the commercial internet, Bezos set out to create an online marketplace for just about anything that could be bought and shipped. Bezos put his future on the line with this daring move, but he sensed the time was right. He named his company Amazon, imagining it as a metaphor for that mighty river, carrying all things from the mountaintops to the oceans of the world. This is reflected in the company logo and its dramatic *A*.

Bezos began modestly enough, establishing one of the internet's first bookselling sites. He saw that many readers were increasing their use of the internet, so books were likely to be one of the first products marketed online. Other early internet entrepreneurs had the same idea about books, but they lacked the vision of Amazon's founder. Books were just his portal into the online world. Once he had established the world's largest bookstore, Bezos quickly expanded Amazon into music, movies, and other entertainment options.

The growth didn't stop there. Eventually the company partnered with thousands of retailers worldwide, offering a global pool of consumers just about anything, from real estate to streaming services. In just over twenty-five years, Amazon has become a great river like its namesake, carrying all things into the global oceans of commerce.

As an internet company that links digital functions with human desires, Amazon has created a business that depends on cutting-edge scientific and technological advances, the latest engineering for its platforms, and instantaneous and accurate mathematical accounting and analysis. Without a workforce trained in basic STEM knowledge, Amazon's success would not be possible, but the company's prosperity also depends on billions of consumers having ready access to its platforms.

The more STEM education consumers have, the more they are likely to use the STEM products and services Amazon sells. STEM-educated consumers earn more, spend more, and increase the size of Amazon's marketplace. As one might expect, the company has stayed ahead of the curve in STEM education, creating access for young, talented students through a program called AWS Educate. The program is billed as an "academic gateway" for young people who plan to work in IT or the cloud.

AWS offers resources for institutions, educators, and students. Educators can receive access to AWS and open-source technologies, as well as training information and access to other educators in the program. Students, ages fourteen and older, can receive credits and training.[50]

There is also a subscription program for STEM toys and games made for younger kids, ages three to thirteen.[51] Each month, the e-commerce giant will send a toy or game that focuses on STEM topics. According to its website, "By making this knowledge more hands-on and engaging, more kids will have access to STEM careers in the future."

Amazon lists the program's services, categorizing them into subsets according to age. This approach gives kids access to STEM problems designed for their level. For the youngest, children ages three to four, the toys and games "introduce simple concepts related to counting, building, and cause and effect." The ones for students from five to seven years feature real experiments with electricity and earth sciences. This is where the first simple math problems come in. Students from third to eighth grades (eight- to thirteen-year-olds) receive "projects and experiments based on principles of physics, chemistry and engineering."

Finally, Amazon's *STEM* earns an *A*. That's the *A* in *STEAM*, which the company gets for including a selection of arts-and-crafts activities "to encourage creativity" and "inspire imagination and innovation in children." The *A* is important. Although STEM skills can

---

50   AWS, "AWS Educate Now."

51   Amazon, "STEM Club."

produce miracles—from internet websites to interstate highways to cures for deadly diseases—their most direct impacts come in the form of material gains.

Science brings new discoveries. Technology turns those discoveries into products and services engineered with mathematical precision. The newly inserted *A* stands for the "art" and inspires all of these processes.

When the concept of STEM education first emerged, programs in the four basic areas answered a crying need, but once educators started developing programs for the classroom, many felt they'd missed one vital subject. That's why even the most basic STEM efforts are now accompanied by a whiff of "STEAM."

Students need access to the arts because the arts are a part of everything. Art might be seen in the design of a new toy, or in a brand-new digital-imaging program, or in the artistic beauty of a building's architecture. It could appear in a traditional painting of a landscape or in a multimedia presentation explaining a business process. Like the other STEM disciplines, art is everywhere. To know our world, we must know art.

EXXON: ENERGY FACTOR

Another company supporting access for "the next generation of STEM talent" is the energy producer ExxonMobil. On its "Energy Factor" page, the company highlights its support for the National Math and Science Initiative (NMSI).[52] The NMSI is a nonprofit organization, which, according to its website, seeks "to advance STEM education to ensure

---

52   ExxonMobil, "Community Engagement."

all students, especially those furthest from opportunity, thrive and reach their highest potential as problem solvers and lifelong learners."

ExxonMobil's website tells readers that it is working within NMSI to "provide tools to the next generation of STEM talent." ExxonMobil's support is helping "schools in the Permian Basin [roughly West Texas and a large part of New Mexico] cultivate future scientists and engineers who may then take advantage of work opportunities in their own backyard."

Among the teachers in the program is Yessica Baiza, who instructs classes in algebra and calculus at a Midland-area high school in West Texas.[53] "There's a real motivation from students who are looking to go into careers like chemical or mechanical engineering," Yessica recently told an interviewer. "The kids are excited about a tough subject. And you see that their parents are excited as well. This momentum helps everyone see the importance of STEM instruction." This is just the kind of approach that encourages accessibility for minority students.

Another STEM teacher, Danelle Morrill of Carlsbad, New Mexico, also saw benefits from the ExxonMobil/NMSI program.[54] "We started project-based learning, which is where you take a real-world situation and apply the science," Morrill said. "The kids were asked to design an air-conditioning system for an outdated recreational center similar to one we have in Carlsbad. They had to take chemistry lessons from the classroom and apply them to figure out how the unit's reactions would take place within that system. The kids got excited because it was a real-world scenario, and they could take STEM concepts and make them relatable to their lives."

These teachers and their students are benefiting from a program designed to increase student participation and improve performance

---

53 Energy Factor, "Nurturing STEM Talent."

54 Energy Factor.

levels. Increases in participation are a primary measurement of access. Whenever possible, the problems students face are ones they will confront in real life.

When students get home, their parents see the difference. After observing a few months of the program, one parent who works in a STEM profession commented, "With three kids in seventh, fifth and first grades enrolled in the Midland school district, they've all grown and matured differently. What's most exciting, as someone working in a technical field, is when I come home, and I see the number of science experiments happening in my house in any given week. As a parent, witnessing the hands-on part of STEM and the growth that comes with it has been a lot of fun."

All of the students in the program strive to qualify for the most advanced classes, where they can develop the necessary skills and apply them in critical thinking. This helps students analyze data in any subject, including history, economics, and other social sciences. Midland School District's Social Sciences Department chair, Megan Gooding, says, "If taught properly, social sciences help in analytical thinking and problem-solving. If you are a doctor or an engineer, having that training and thinking is essential. Your math skills are important, but social sciences can give students a leg up in their STEM careers since they will have a different set of skills to pull from."[55]

Gooding gives a lot of credit to the ExxonMobil/NMSI program and expects to see even more improvements in her students' access to higher education in the future. "At our school, I expect NMSI to help [improve test] scores. I think we will see students getting into colleges that kids from West Texas typically don't get into. If we continue to push and stay right here on the cutting edge, maybe some of our students can go to Harvard."

---

55 Energy Factor.

For students like those in Gooding's classes, the future is bright. Their newly gained access to STEM learning tools gives them advantages they will need throughout their lives. Lazaro Cosma, Exxon's operations manager in Midland, put it well, saying, "Programs like NMSI get the tools and training into the hands of our educators.... When we're seeing individuals come into the workforce, it really is about having that strong foundation and developing critical thinkers. From new interns to professionals who've been with the company for years, it comes down to how they're able to think through and solve problems.... STEM education is foundational to building that."[56]

> *People need access to STEM skills and data throughout their lives.*

Most of what we've discussed here concerning access, diversity, and equity has been about kids in classrooms. That's where most STEM education begins, but it doesn't end there. People need access to STEM skills and data throughout their lives. We can see this in the public sector where cooperative STEM efforts, such as those of the USDA and our nation's HBCUs, are coming together. We saw an example of HBCUs in the last chapter in Delaware State University and its president, longtime Biden advisor Tony Allen.

---

56 Energy Factor.

THE LEGACY OF BLACK FRATERNITIES AND SORORITIES AT HBCUs

HBCUs are at the forefront of the movement to provide STEM access to minority students. One HBCU president, Tennessee State University's Dr. Glenda Glover, wrote an article for prnewswire.com noting that the administration's Build Back Better initiative "includes a $5 billion increase in funding ... which can be used by HBCUs, tribal colleges and universities (TCUs), and MSIs [minority-serving institutions] to strengthen their academic, administrative, and fiscal capabilities, including creating or expanding educational programs in high-demand fields (e.g., STEM, computer sciences, nursing, and allied health). Build Back Better would direct an additional $2 billion toward building a pipeline of skilled healthcare workers with graduate degrees from HBCUs, TCUs, and MSIs."[57]

Dr. Glover is also the international president of Alpha Kappa Alpha Sorority, Inc. (AKA), and her interest in STEM access and diversity parallels that of AKA.[58] Sororities and fraternities like hers bring friendly competition to STEM efforts, producing benefits for all the students who follow.

One fraternity whose members have brought great energy and talent to STEM education is Alpha Phi Alpha (APA). Its general president is Willis Lonzer III, whose interest in STEM is a natural fit for all his specialties. He has earned degrees in chemistry, biochemistry, physiology, and biophysics.[59]

---

57   Glover, "White House Continues."

58   Alpha Kappa Alpha, "About AKA."

59   Voorhees College, "Voorhees College Prepares."

According to one recent biographical article, Dr. Lonzer "has 20 years of global corporate experience having held positions in global research and development with AstraZeneca, the Ortho Biotech division of Johnson & Johnson Pharmaceuticals, and global medical affairs divisions of Abbott Laboratories, AbbVie Inc., and Shire Pharmaceuticals. He currently serves as regional director at Horizon Therapeutics where he is involved in identifying research partnerships and strategic drug development opportunities for marketed and pipeline assets."[60]

Lonzer and Glover are just two of the many proponents of STEM diversity, inclusion, access, and equity who are also proud members of America's majority-Black fraternities and sororities. Several of the people cited in this book are members of Lonzer's Alpha Phi Alpha fraternity, including Houston's Mayor Sylvester Turner and Congressman Bobby Scott. They follow in the footsteps of legendary members such as Dr. Martin Luther King Jr., W. E. B. Du Bois, Justice Thurgood Marshall, Jesse Owens, Andrew Young, Duke Ellington, and Quincy Jones.

STEM AND ACCESS DURING THE PANDEMIC

Like anything else, STEM education has been affected by the pandemic. One of these impacts came in response to the two million newly unemployed Texas residents in the spring of 2020. That's when the USDA joined with Prairie View A&M University (PVAM) to create a virtual training program that could be accessed remotely. USDA Extension agents helped 1,500 people learn ways to improve

60   Voorhees College.

their job search and professional skills.[61] In surveys for this program, researchers found whole communities lacking consistent access to broadband service.

As they identified the particular needs of each area, PVAM added a loan-packaging program for strapped local business owners and entrepreneurs. This gave them access to CARES Act COVID-19 relief funds. According to program representatives, "Ninety-two small business owners have participated in the training series and received more than $500,000 in loans and grants. Participants have applied for another $333,000 in business grants."

Before we can achieve diversity, or find equity, we must have access. To help minority students and workers gain access, institutions and organizations must open their programs and design them to welcome anyone with an interest in developing STEM knowledge and skills. Corporations, schools, and government agencies need to cooperate in their efforts to spread access to anyone who has a stake in the process. Once that access is established, we must then solve the problem of inclusion, which is coming up next.

---

61   Cotton, "PVAMU Receives $500,000."

CHAPTER 5

PIONEERS!
THE COURAGE TO BE FIRST

Hand in hand with access comes inclusion, an idea as broad as the people it serves. A teacher might have access to course materials and a classroom. But will she include all interested students in her program? Will she promote her class to students from different backgrounds? Or will she simply wait and see if someone shows interest? This is the kind of situation where pioneers are needed.

A pioneering teacher won't be limited to conventional methods. She'll have the courage to innovate and break down barriers. Pioneering students will be those brave young people whose desire to learn is greater than their fear of the pressures of being first. This can be true of pioneers in classrooms, schools, and whole school systems.

Size is not a determinant. Inclusion can apply in all kinds of situations. Different players will have different motivations. School systems want to be included in all the funding and materials available from all sources. Individual schools want to be included in beneficial programs and policies. Teachers want to be included in their schools' decision-making processes. Students want to be included in good classes, sports teams, and other school activities.

This is true of all systems, schools, teachers, and students, but it's most important for those students who are disadvantaged. Dark skin or a foreign accent shouldn't exclude anyone from STEM programs, but that's what has happened in the past. If we practice the principle of inclusion, we can avoid that pitfall now and in the future.

Inclusion brings together all students, whatever their skin color or background, giving everyone a role in the learning experience. In STEM education, this means including every student in classroom discussions, research groups, laboratory teams, physical experiments, and other projects. Students from different backgrounds should be encouraged to work together, to allot tasks, and to share their discoveries with each other.

This is true throughout our schools, including colleges and universities. In a paper published on the website of the National Institute of Health, Tess L. Killpack and Laverne C. Melón wrote, "It is becoming clear that, as institutions of higher education increase compositional diversity, they must also ensure that they cultivate intellectual and social environments where all students have the opportunity to achieve academic success."[62]

So, we must create and cultivate environments that encourage inclusion. It's one thing to bring minority students into a mostly white

---

62   Killpack and Melón, "Toward Inclusive STEM Classrooms."

student body, but it is another to encourage them to use that access to take STEM courses.

Killpack and Melón went on to analyze the problem statistically, finding that

- in the past thirty-five years, the percentage of Latino college students increased from 4% to 15%;

- in the same period, the percentage of Black college students went from 10% to 15%;

- in the past decade, the number of enrolled students over age twenty-five rose by 35%; and

- 20% of Latino students and 40% of Black students who intended to major in the natural sciences in their first year of college did not earn natural sciences degrees, while among white and Asian students, this loss is 1.5% and 7% respectively.[63]

This paints a picture of minority students setting out on an academic path toward degrees in STEM subjects but then drifting away in surprisingly high numbers a year or two later. Why? Citing a study published in *Education Researcher*, Emily Arnim of EAB.com goes into these numbers more deeply, writing that "this is the result of a combination of students changing majors and students choosing to leave college. More than a third of Black (40%) and Latino (37%) students switch majors before earning a degree, compared with 29% of white STEM students. Another 26% of Black STEM students and 20% of Latino STEM students drop out of college altogether—13 and

---

63   Killpack and Melón.

7 percentage points higher, respectively, than white STEM students (13%), according to the study."[64]

THE CONSEQUENCES OF EXCLUSION

Some of this loss of interest is due to a lack of STEM courses in grades K–12. Often students' interest can be revived through tutoring or in a remedial course, but a lot of this decline comes from the negative feelings that often ignite when someone is faced with bigotry. Arnim quotes Deana Crouser, a Latina who began as a chemical engineering major at the University of Washington. "I spent too much time in my head feeling like I didn't belong or wasn't smart enough, that I couldn't concentrate on my work," Crouser told Arnim. In the end, it was too much, and Crouser decided to find a new major.[65]

This young woman might have stayed in STEM were it not for the lack of encouragement and feelings of inferiority that seemed to be built into the system. The damage done by these problems could be repaired, or entirely avoided, if these courses already had more minority students. As Arnim writes, "Students tend to gravitate toward majors where the majority of students look like them." We should note that this is also true about the number of minority teachers.

This problem also goes back to a time long before college. Even in the early grades of K–12, teachers tend to exclude certain groups from various STEM activities. American education is still caught in sexist and racist traditions. Young girls still feel encouraged to con-

---

64 Arnim, "A Third of Minority Students."

65 Arnim.

centrate on arts, literature, and clerical skills, while young Black males are often channeled into trade courses and sports. Those who show STEM talents would only need a slight push to convince them that they should use their educations to refine those talents into more profitable (and often more inspiring) professions.

In 2018 the Pew Research Center reported that while Black workers made up 11% of the US workforce, in the STEM professions that was only 9%.[66] They also found that women are underrepresented in STEM, where the gender wage gap is higher than it is in other occupations.

INSTITUTIONS FOCUSED ON INCLUSION

StatePress.com's Luke Chatham reported a story on STEM programs at Arizona State University, writing that an "ASU research center was created [in 2020] to help forge a more inclusive STEM education for students.[67]" Chatham tells readers, "The Research for Inclusive STEM Education (RISE) Center aims to achieve that goal through the undergraduate experience within science, technology, engineering, and math. The center examines inequities within classrooms, research labs and learning environments to create interventions."

Chatham cites Sara Brownell, director of RISE, who said that different people have different experiences in the classroom based on their identity, but she also contended that identity alone doesn't explain this difference. "The identity isn't causing the difference," Brownell told her listeners. "The difference exists, and it shouldn't

---

66   Funk and Parker, "Diversity in the STEM Workforce."

67   Chatham, "New Research Center."

be there. STEM has historically been more white, more male and has been much less accepting about sharing people's identity. People have cared less in STEM about identity, and that's where we can make the biggest impact since that's where some of the biggest potential problems are."

The center's associate director, Kristen Parrish, told Chatham that creating changes in STEM would help the university change in bigger ways. "This is really how we can help ASU achieve its own goals," she said.[68]

On the other side of the country, in another effort to bolster STEM initiatives, the Pittsburgh Post-Gazette (PPG) Foundation announced the creation of a $20 million STEM program in early 2021.[69] According to a *Post-Gazette* article by Joyce Gannon, the money will fund "after-school programs for STEM, career and mentoring opportunities, as well as support for social justice initiatives such as criminal justice reform."

Malesia Dunn, the PPG Foundation's executive director, cited the "urgent need for educating people around STEM—particularly Black people and other People of Color." On the PPG website, Dunn adds, "We aim to reach diverse students and communities to champion change and empower historically underrepresented populations with greater opportunities to achieve brighter futures. Through this important commitment, we will prioritize equity and justice within education to close the racial gaps in STEM learning and careers, and help our society meet collective challenges quickly, creatively, and effectively."

The PPG program is designed to foster inclusion. One initiative is in partnership with local Boys & Girls Clubs. Aimed at teens in disadvantaged neighborhoods, this program trains kids to work with

---

68 Chatham.

69 Gannon, "PPG Commits."

artificial intelligence systems, helping minority young people develop vital skills for the future. Girls are specifically targeted in an after-school STEM program at Pittsburgh's Neighborhood Academy.[70]

One very visible PPG STEM event occurred on August 17, 2021, when more than two hundred students and parents attended Science at Play at PPG Paints Arena. There the PPG Foundation partnered with Carnegie Science Center and the Pittsburgh Penguins Foundation to sponsor an afternoon of STEM activities.[71]

The PPG website described it as "an immersive experience for Pittsburgh-area youth to learn about Science, Technology, Engineering and Math (STEM) in the game of hockey at the home of the Pittsburgh Penguins. The event was free of charge and provided an opportunity for several local nonprofit organizations to share the experience with their students—including students from Gwen's Girls and STEM Coding Lab." Summing up the event and its goals, Malesia Dunn said, "We believe that education enables possibilities and progress that lead to brighter futures and a better world for all, and together with our nonprofit partners, we aim to help inspire next-generation innovators in the areas of robotics, mobility, color science, chemistry, engineering, and more."[72]

PPG's STEM program will extend and continue these activities, supporting them with funds and organizing expertise. Included in the package is a gift to the Advanced Leadership Initiative, which is helping Black STEM professionals find places in the region's executive suites. There are also funds supporting Pittsburgh's Latino Community Center. Most of this money is slated to put laptops into the hands of

---

70   Gannon.

71   Education, PPG Foundation, "PPG Brings STEM Learning."

72   Education, PPG Foundation.

needy students who have been forced into remote learning situations throughout the pandemic shutdown.

Inclusion is at the heart of all these programs. Inclusion guarantees that problems in diversity, equity, and access will be addressed. Once we include everyone and have real diversity, students will reflect their regions and origins. If we give them all the same opportunities, they will have equity and access. It sounds easy, but the wait has been long—long enough to nurture latent racism and other obstacles.

MINORITY STEM PIONEERS

To overcome these obstacles, schools must find ways to recruit minority STEM students and make their programs more welcoming. In "How to Recruit and Retain Underrepresented Minorities," Ashanti Johnson and Melanie Harrison Okoro examine the roots of the inclusion problem.[73] Johnson serves as vice provost for faculty recruitment at the University of Texas at Arlington, and she's also the executive director of the Institute for Broadening Participation. In 2010 Johnson won the Presidential Medal for Excellence in Science, Mathematics, and Engineering. Okoro is a water-quality specialist with the National Oceanic and Atmospheric Administration who has the extensive title of National Marine Fisheries Service West Region Aquatic Invasive Species Coordinator.

As a young, pioneering student in the Oak Cliff area of Dallas in the early 1980s, Johnson was inspired by an early STEM education program that was open to minority children like her.[74] "I was given

---

73   Johnson and Okoro, "How to Recruit."

74   Yates, "Meet Dr. Ashanti Johnson."

a class assignment as part of my school's talented and gifted program to identify a career that I wanted to pursue and then to conduct independent research on it," Johnson writes. "For me, that was easy: I wanted to be the 'next' Jacques Cousteau. I watched the TV icon and oceanographer on PBS almost every Saturday. He worked with people of various nationalities, who spoke with different accents, as they explored exotic underwater locations. Inspired by his program, each year from third through twelfth grade, I conducted a new independent project related to the ocean."

Although her parents and teachers knew little or nothing about oceanography, they encouraged young Ashanti, helping her in any way they could. She writes, "My family and teachers instilled in me the belief that if I applied myself, I could achieve my career goal. They also taught me that it was important to be successful so that I could give back to the community and help others achieve." Ashanti Johnson went on with her studies, eventually becoming one of the top ocean scientists of the last half century. In the article, she writes, "As I reflect on my career, I see that the encouragement within my community and the educational programs I had were essential to my believing in myself enough to stay the course through the arduous journey of learning how to do research."

The young Melanie Harrison Okoro daydreamed of becoming a surgeon, but she couldn't slice in a straight line, even on her kitchen cutting board, much less in an operating room. Besides, she fainted at the sight of blood. Nonetheless, Okoro felt the attractions of scientific inquiry. "As a child I had loved swimming and fishing with my great-grandmother and twin sister in Lake Martin in Alabama," she writes. "During my undergraduate studies, those childhood experiences led me back to the water, into my career as an environmental scientist for NOAA Fisheries."[75]

When Okoro entered a PhD program in Maryland, she met Dr. Johnson. Okoro had never known an oceanographer, and certainly not an African American woman oceanographer. Together their careers illustrate the advantages that diversity, inclusion, equity, access, and mentorship can give. Using their combined experience, these women have arrived at some conclusions about STEM education.

"The proportion of underrepresented minorities in science and engineering would need to triple or quadruple to match their share of the overall U.S. population," Johnson and Okoro write. "Peers, mentors, and accessible educational programming—like that offered to talented and gifted students [in school], or outside of school, like Cousteau's TV show—were essential to our development as scientists. To help retain minority students in the STEM majors to which they aspire, we believe it's important that currently successful programs be examined and bolstered, and such practices encouraged in the communities and institutions where they are most needed."

> *The proportion of underrepresented minorities in science and engineering would need to triple or quadruple to match their share of the overall U.S. population.*

---

75   Wikimedia Foundation, "Melanie Harrison Okoro."

The authors cite several STEM efforts, whose sponsors include the National Oceanic and Atmospheric Administration (NOAA) and Savannah State University (SSU). They write that these programs "were designed to help students see themselves in and prepare for marine science research, management, and public policy careers via three K–12 outreach and exposure programs: Coast Camp, the National Ocean Sciences Bowl regional Southern Stingray Bowl, and SSU Ocean Ambassadors."

The authors show that these programs are models of inclusion, writing, "About 50 percent of the K–12 students who interact with the Ambassadors are from underrepresented minority groups.... The Center's K–12 outreach activities engage about 1,200 diverse local K–12 students annually. Many minority participants go on to pursue marine science degrees." This kind of result would be impossible without inclusion.[76]

As the authors finish their essay, they remain optimistic, writing, "Since its initial participation in the educational center in 2001, SSU has done an outstanding job of providing hands-on science exposure activities for K–12 underrepresented minority students, while also facilitating professional development opportunities for their students. For many of the K–12 students, the SSU programs are their first exposure to marine science."

Johnson and Okoro are passing forward gifts that were seen only rarely in their generation. Johnson was born at the end of the civil rights movement, when interest in STEM education was just beginning to coalesce, largely among affluent and mostly white educators. Attention to STEM education for Black people was scant to nonexistent. Johnson benefited from a pioneering program unavail-

---

76 Johnson and Okoro, "How to Recruit."

able to most of the minority children of her generation. She was included when few other minority children had that chance.

Okoro was born fifteen years later, in the 1980s. By the time she reached school age, STEM education was an idea whose time had come, but the first schools that got it were still the affluent, mostly white institutions. As happened with so many other educational advances, minority inclusion in STEM came only as an afterthought.

Nevertheless, Johnson, Okoro, and other minority students of their eras did what they had to do. Once they were included, they took full advantage of that, studying, excelling, and finally producing some of the best work in their STEM field. Theirs is also a story of mentorship, and that story will start the next chapter.

CHAPTER 6

GIANTS!
STANDING ON
THEIR SHOULDERS

Dr. Johnson and Dr. Okoro were pioneers, and so they were often the first women—or first Black people, or both—to do the things they did. Dr. Johnson's path to higher academic degrees was marked by firsts. "In 1993, I became the first African American to receive a marine science B.S. degree from Texas A&M University at Galveston," she told an audience at a recent forum. "Six years later, I became the first African American to receive a doctoral degree in chemical oceanography from Texas A&M."[77]

She went on to note that while these were achievements well worth celebrating, her listeners should consider just a few of the obstacles

---

77   Bland, "Ashanti Johnson."

she'd faced. Though it had been thirty years since Dr. Johnson started college, she recalled that "the last time I attended a class with another African American student or was taught by an African American was in high school." This brilliant woman had gone through college and an extensive postgraduate academic career in oceanography without any official instruction or formal mentorship from anyone who looked like her or even had much in common with her. It's easy to see that most of her career has been a lonely road.

Dr. Johnson had always displayed a talent for science, and she felt the calling of oceanography as early as third grade, but she later wrote, "It was not until twelfth grade that I learned of Dr. Ernest Everett Just, an African American marine scientist who died in 1941. Despite the absence of contemporary African American role models, I was determined to make positive contributions to the geosciences." Although she had to search for minority mentors, Johnson did have help from home.

Her grandmother and her parents believed in her, and that faith fueled her dreams. They instilled self-confidence in this talented child and taught her that the more help she needed, the more she would need to help others succeed. It was a philosophy of pay-it-forward. "This belief and sense of responsibility remain and influence my actions," she told her forum audience.

According to a younger colleague, one of the many whom Johnson mentored, "Ashanti has been a stalwart advocate for supporting underrepresented youth who reflect talent in STEM professions, especially in the geosciences." This colleague calls Johnson "a stellar role model," recognizing how the oceanographer "continued her research in marine science, while pursuing the professional development of students and building diversity initiatives in STEM through the integration of research and education."[78]

THE IMPORTANCE OF STEM MENTORSHIP

In an online post, Melanie Harrison Okoro has described herself as a "fisherwoman, new mom … and a Baltimore Ravens fan." Both she and Johnson have written extensively about inclusion in STEM fields, and they have also spoken out about the nature of, and need for, mentorship.

Mentorship plays a role in almost all professional development. Mentors provide experience, analysis, and wisdom to students and youthful colleagues. Mentorship is built into some jobs, including teaching. Teachers give students information, but they also teach them how to think. A good teacher looks at each student's potential, then searches for ways to help that student achieve it. That's what good mentors do too.

Parents, counselors, and friends are often mentors, but their advice tends to be about personal issues. When they mentor us on work in a specialty they know little about, their feedback is usually general and supportive. They are good cheerleaders, but they seldom have any answers about our specialties. So, who should we turn to when we're confronted with issues in our work?

An older, more experienced colleague can be a valuable professional mentor. Often, bosses are mentors. Even if the employees know more about their individual areas of expertise, a good boss knows how

---

78 Bland.

all those skills fit together. A good mentor can help a coworker step back from confusing details and see the larger picture.

Okoro first met Johnson in 2009, when Okoro was studying at the University of Maryland, Baltimore County (UMBC). "I was a PhD student," Okoro said in a recent interview posted on YouTube. "I spent a lot of hours working in wetlands and urban streams. A lot of that work is done in isolation." She brought this up with another student, adding that she would like to meet more African American students like herself. Okoro's fellow student suggested that she investigate Dr. Johnson and her program. This friend, who knew Johnson and was familiar with her work, seemed to think Okoro would be a good fit for the program.

Okoro saw that Johnson had designed the program for talented minority students like herself. It was aimed at graduate students in degree programs in the earth sciences, which was obvious from its long but descriptive title: Minorities Striving and Pursuing Higher Degrees of Success in Earth System Science (MS PHD'S). When Okoro learned of the fine results the program's students were reporting, she wanted in. Although she failed in her first attempt, the second time she tried, Johnson accepted her application.

Smart, well-organized, and hard-working—Okoro was just the kind of student Johnson was looking for. "When I meet talented people, I want them to be engaged," Johnson says. "You need a community that supports you, so you won't feel so isolated." From her own experience, she understood that support is a basic ingredient in the foundation of mentorship.

BEING FIRST IS BEING CHALLENGED

Anyone who believes in you can offer you this kind of spiritual mentoring, but sometimes we need help from someone who knows and appreciates our work. We crave the opinions of respected professionals, even if they are critical—sometimes particularly when they're critical. We want to know what we're doing right and what we're doing wrong. We see examples of this every day in sports. Sports have long traditions of mentorship, as older players teach young novices how to survive and thrive.

Veterans know the game, and all its ins and outs. Younger athletes must take advantage of this to achieve their full potential. In team sports, this process is obvious—with managers, coaches, and team captains all built into the structure—but it is also true in individual games, like tennis and golf. Coaching plays a huge part in the development of nearly all sports skills.

The problem of mentorship and minorities was obvious over seventy years ago for one of baseball's greatest Hall of Famers: Jackie Robinson. When Robinson first broke the color line, beginning the integration of the white major leagues, he was more isolated than any baseball player had ever been. It's one of the twentieth century's greatest stories, with highlights that have been covered in movies, documentaries, and books.[79]

As the first African American to play in the white leagues of the nation's preeminent sport (baseball was then referred to as "the national pastime"), Robinson knew his story would go down in history. Whether it would be a story of hope or a story of shattered

---

79 Polin, "A Legacy of Breaking Barriers."

dreams was completely dependent on him. He had to be great, or his failure would become a failure of Black folks everywhere.

Even when Robinson earned a regular spot in the lineup, some of his white teammates would barely speak to him. Opposing pitchers aimed fastballs at his head, and when he got on base, the infielders taunted him with ugly slurs. More than one infielder spiked him whenever the opportunity arose.

A consummate base runner, one of Robinson's signature skills was stealing bases. When he would slide into second base, sometimes the white player covering the bag would shove a spiked heel into Robinson's ankle. This only stopped when Robinson started making a habit of getting up, brushing himself off, and stealing third base. More than once, he even stole home—another skill opponents learned to fear.

Many white fans refused to believe in his talents. They shouted the worst racial epithets and even spit on him. Black fans turned out in droves to see him, but in those segregated times, they were often required to sit in distant sections of the stadiums in the bleacher seats. Robinson, who played second base, was lucky to hear any of their cheers above the white curses.

MENTORSHIP BEYOND BASEBALL

One of the biggest reasons Jackie Robinson's road was so difficult was the lack of Black mentors in the white major leagues. As Ashanti Johnson and many others would learn in the following decades, being first is being challenged. When we are challenged, we feel the need for allies—but Robinson had to stand alone. With so many coaches and players ostracizing him because of his race, Robinson had few friendly faces he could turn to, even in the dugout. Those who supported him were white, and though their intentions came from the heart, they couldn't fully understand the effects of racism. They didn't realize that Robinson was fighting a battle that spanned lifetimes.

Robinson responded by playing better and better baseball. He soon became one of the greatest success stories in sports history. He won the National League's Rookie of the Year award, and three years later an almost all-white press corps voted him the National League's Most Valuable Player. By that time, Robinson's Dodgers had added three more Black faces.[80] Those players had the luxury of the first experienced Black mentor in the white major leagues: Jackie Robinson. He didn't let them down. In 1955, with Robinson still leading them, the Dodgers won their first World Series ever, ending decades of postseason defeats.

With stars like the incomparable Don Newcombe, Jim Gilliam, and future Hall of Famer Roy Campanella, these Brooklyn World Champions had more Players of Color than any other team in the formerly all-white major leagues. The Dodgers and other Black players were introducing a whole new style of baseball. They brought it from the Negro Leagues where the game was played with a style and verve unknown in the white major leagues. They played with passion, guile, and speed, making every play more exciting, as they rescued major league baseball from impending oblivion. Once Robinson had broken the sport's color line, the young teammates he had mentored obliterated it—though only on the field.

Robinson's mentorship had effects beyond the baseball diamond. He mentored all Americans by demonstrating the importance of courage, honesty, and endurance. In 1957, a decade after Robinson

---

80 Steverson, "Jackie Robinson's Life."

first stepped onto a major league baseball diamond, nine young Black students were chosen to integrate Little Rock's Central High School.[81] When violence loomed, their supporters urged them to "be like Jackie." Cementing this thought was a phone call from Jackie himself. When these teenagers had to stand up to curses, spittle, and assault, they remembered Robinson's inspiring voice, as well as his stoic bravery and endurance in the face of similar dangers.

The Little Rock Nine weren't just any teenagers. Just as Robinson had been selected by the Dodgers because of his superior talents, these nine young people all had established fine academic records. As one of them, Carlotta Walls LaNier, later recalled, "I think what took place was that we were checked for our grades, our character, our community involvement, our church going—I call it the Jackie Robinson test."[82]

The Nine went on to professional careers, including some in STEM-related areas.[83] Gloria Ray's bachelor's degree was in chemistry and mathematics, and she had a distinguished career in computer sciences. Thelma Mothershed earned two advanced degrees and taught high school courses in home sciences for twenty-eight years. Terrence Roberts earned postgraduate degrees in sociology, social welfare, and psychology and taught those subjects throughout his working life. In 1993, as interest in inclusion, access, and diversity took root, President Clinton appointed Little Rock Nine member Minnijean Brown as deputy assistant secretary for workforce diversity in the Department of the Interior.

---

81 Original Sources, "Jackie Robinson, President Eisenhower."

82 Whitcomb, "Carlotta Walls LaNier."

83 National Park Service, "The Little Rock Nine."

A PIONEER FROM AMERICA'S "MURDER CAPITAL"

Jackie Robinson inspired millions, but the people he helped most of all were the pioneers. There were the famous ones who he influenced personally, like the Little Rock Nine, but there were countless others, like David Northern, a pioneer in public housing.[84]

Northern grew up in Gary, Indiana, when it was known as America's "murder capital." He went to Ball State University, then on to a career in public housing authorities in the Midwest and the South. Throughout his career, Northern has been a trailblazer, often being the first African American to fill a position of responsibility and authority.

In an odd twist, Northern became mentor to fellow Ball State student Taryl Bonds. Bonds also came from Gary, but he'd emerged from a more affluent background. Bonds was impressed with Northern's growing drive. "I could tell that David was beginning to focus and buckle down," he says now. Northern got his first job in public housing and eventually suggested that Bonds follow him into that field, which Bonds did.

Since then, Northern has promoted many improvements for the lives of public housing residents in Lake County, Illinois; Birmingham, Alabama; and now Houston. These include educational and training programs anchored in STEM skills. Northern is happy to be a pioneer standing on a giant's (Jackie Robinson's) shoulders, but he wants tomorrow's Black professionals to be able to focus on pioneering advances in STEM fields.

---

84   TAAHP, "David A. Northern Sr."

In 2016, forty-three years after Jackie Robinson's premature death from cancer, *Knoxville News Sentinel* columnist W. R. "Bryan" Steverson wrote, "The Rev. Martin Luther King Jr. called [Robinson] the founder of the civil rights movement."[85] In a recent interview, filmmaker Ken Burns, who produced *Jackie Robinson*, said, "One could argue Robinson was one of the five or six greatest Americans of all time."[86] By living his life the way he did, this baseball great inspired generations of young people to believe that anything might be possible.

When his career on the field was over, Robinson spent the sixteen years he had left championing civil rights for all People of Color. His own experience gave him a deep understanding of the obstacles Black folks face in education and the workplace. Though Jackie had been a good student in college, his family's financial constraints had prevented him from completing his degree requirements. Now he was helping young Black scholars stay in school.

After Jackie died, his wife, Rachel, kept the faith, establishing the Jackie Robinson Foundation in 1973. As the foundation's website tells it, "Rachel Robinson started the foundation soon after Jackie's death, as she understood the value of higher education in lifting individuals, along with their families. She herself had earned bachelor and master's degrees in nursing and eventually taught at Yale and other institutions."[87] The foundation's primary effort is its Scholars program, which started out of the Robinsons' Stamford, Connecticut, living room.

The website describes this as a "hands-on, four-year program including peer and professional mentoring, internship placements, leadership training, travel and community service opportunities,

---

85   Steverson, "Journey to Justice."

86   Keveney, "Ken Burns: Jackie Robinson."

87   Jackie Robinson Foundation, "Explore Our Roots."

practical life skills development, and networking opportunities." Since it began in that living room forty-three years ago, the program has given scholarships and support totaling more than $85 million.

MENTORSHIP: ANCIENT ADVICE, MODERN NECESSITY

In chapter 3, we met Dr. Shirley Malcom, pioneering Black scientist and prolific mentor. In 2019 the American Association for the Advancement of Science (AAAS) published "STEM Mentoring: Emerging Strategies for Inclusion."[88] In her preface to that essay, Dr. Malcom began with an example of mentoring from the legendary character the practice is named for, in one of the oldest stories on earth:

> In Homer's *Odyssey*, Mentor is a friend of Odysseus who was placed in the role of guardian and guide to his son, Telemachus, when Odysseus went off to the Trojan War. It is also said that Athena, Greek goddess of wisdom (and courage, war, inspiration, mathematics, strength, strategy, arts, crafts and more) would assume the form of Mentor when she would appear to Telemachus to offer counsel. Though his father was not present, Telemachus received wisdom and knowledge to help him navigate through life.

The publication goes on to describe ongoing mentoring programs for minority STEM professionals at the National Institutes of Health, the National Science Foundation, and the US Department of Agriculture.

---

88   AAAS, "STEM Mentoring."

Its authors note that the push for educational diversity in STEM programs has "improved the participation of underrepresented and underserved minorities, women, and persons with disabilities in STEM education and careers." But it also notes that "progress has been slow and insufficient to meet the demands of the US STEM workforce…. As a result, educational leaders from around the country have sought to identify proven methods of supporting students to help them develop STEM skills in all learning environments."[89]

This recognizes that the most effective mentoring begins early— when tomorrow's STEM professionals are still in school. Women, People of Color, and other minority students form their attitudes about work and its potential early. Often this is when a young person's world either opens, welcoming new ideas, or closes down, discouraging the young person from any further real learning.

A mentor can ease this process and help young students overcome obstacles, while encouraging them to rise to meet challenges. This is especially true when a student is the only minority within a classroom, as Dr. Ashanti Johnson was. What Dr. Johnson lacked was a good mentor who could advise her on the best tactics for neutralizing racist attitudes and prioritizing tasks to solve problems.

ACTION ITEMS FOR MINORITY MENTORSHIP

The AAAS authors reach several conclusions and offer some solutions, starting with the inclusion of "women and those from other under-represented groups" in leadership training. They also recommend

89 AAAS.

recruiting more minority candidates to mentor these groups. Among their "Action Items," they list

- hire more STEM teachers and faculty from underrepresented groups to help make institutions feel more welcoming and relevant to all students; and

- provide mentors and mentees with integrated training so that both parties understand what constitutes good mentoring, including regular and sustained one-on-one interactions, integration of inspiration, guidance, and the connection to opportunities.[90]

Their "Next Steps" include the following:

- invest in long-term professional development for faculty, staff, and administrators and embed mentoring in learning environments from the beginning (in classrooms, labs, etc.) rather than as an add-on later; and

- secure well-defined commitments for sustainability of mentoring programs as part of the grant-review process and promote the institutionalization of existing ones.

These items and steps highlight the main issues in creating, growing, and *maintaining* high-quality mentoring for minorities. The

> *Empathy. That's what minority mentors can bring to the minority students and professionals they are coaching.*

---

90 AAAS.

AAAS is putting this emphasis on student mentoring because the things that happen in school shape our approach to the problems we see in the workplace.[91]

In all these examples, the mentors understand the unique problems of the people they are mentoring because they've dealt with the same issues in their own careers. Dr. Johnson recognized something of herself in Melanie Harrison Okoro. Jackie Robinson saw the long fight ahead of those nine brave students in Little Rock. Dr. Malcom has used her own educational history to connect with today's young minority STEM students. Each of these is an example of empathy. That's what minority mentors can bring to the minority students and professionals they are coaching.

UNIQUE CHALLENGES IN TROUBLING TIMES

Our own difficult times have presented unique problems in the mentoring process. In 2020, as COVID restrictions raised new questions and possibilities about what kind of work could be done online, a study emerged looking at the quality of online mentoring, with attention on minority mentoring. Researchers at the University of Massachusetts Amherst ran an experiment using an online mutual mentoring model they've named "Amplifying Voice." The lead author, Sandra Petersen, is a professor of veterinary and animal sciences, and she worked with coauthors Barbara Pearson, recently retired from the

---

91　AAAS.

Office of Research, and Mary Moriarty of Research and Evaluation Associates in Northampton, Massachusetts.[92]

These coauthors cite sources showing that minority women are nearly 18% of the population, but they are only 3% of the tenure-track STEM faculty in four-year colleges and universities. They go on to note that mentoring is the common thread in helping young academics achieve success and that this is especially important for minorities in STEM disciplines. These young professionals need input from people who have had the same kinds of experiences they are facing. Yet these minority workers are the ones who are least likely to get effective, empathetic mentoring.

A June 2020 article at the Phys.org website describes how Petersen and her colleagues recruited and organized groups at twenty universities. All members participated in sixty- to ninety-minute every-other-week Zoom meetings. All filled out a presurvey questionnaire, then fourteen months later, they did a postsurvey questionnaire.[93] The authors found that "participants generally agreed that the components of the mutual mentoring model, as well as the way it was instituted and supported, were effective."

Notably, 86% of these professionals were positive about the results. According to the report, these participants felt that "the format met mentoring needs and provided an effective platform for discussing challenges faced in their institutions; 92% indicated that it was also a good place for discussing solutions to those challenges. Also 93% agreed or strongly agreed that the virtual environment was an effective way to conduct a mentoring group."

Each group began by choosing a facilitator. At the end of the study, these facilitators believed that their groups had worked well

---

92   University of Massachusetts Amherst, "Women Faculty in STEM."

93   University of Massachusetts Amherst.

because they understood one another's struggles and realized they weren't alone, and they "often came to new insights by sharing professional experiences, achievements and challenges."

The authors concluded that their experiment was a success, writing, "We believe that the Amplifying Voices program is an attractive model for providing a mentoring community for underrepresented minority women."

Empathy and experience are the keys to mentoring. We find them in every example, experiment, and survey. That is why it's so essential for every minority STEM student who goes on to achieve success to eventually pay it forward and to mentor students and young colleagues. First and foremost, aspiring students must see that it can be done!

CHAPTER 7

UNITED!
THE MAGICAL MULTIPLYING EFFECT OF COLLABORATION

We live and work in an economy that thrives on competition. Individuals compete to provide more and better products and services to an ever-growing consumer base. Workers try to do a better job than their coworkers, and companies vie with other companies to earn more of our dollars. We measure success by yardsticks of quality and profits, but if we're investing in a company's future or hiring the company's future CEO, we want to know they can compete. If a person or team can survive a battle, learn its lessons, and rise, ready to fight another day, we recognize that as a valuable credential.

Americans regard competitiveness as a national trait, leading some to enshrine it above all other values. They will correctly assert that competition built our country, as well as the rest of the developed world. A system that encourages sensible competition in the search for customers can result in more and better products and services.

Competing automakers give us a wider array of choices every year, increasing safety and efficiency while creating a relaxing comfort zone for our ride. Competing restaurants search for tastes, textures, and experiences that will please us. Competing builders put up better houses, and competing communications companies increase the speed and clarity of our phone calls, emails, and texts.

But competition won't get us anywhere unless it is accompanied by collaboration. I'm talking about the kind of collaboration we find on a team, where each member integrates his or her talents into the team's pursuit of a common goal. In STEM education and other STEM pursuits, collaboration happens all the time. Of course, it builds bridges, but it also brings inclusion, which fosters diversity. Without collaboration, STEM education loses much of its potential benefit.

TEAM SPORTS: COMPETITION + COLLABORATION

One of the most obvious examples of competition is also one of collaboration: team sports. The sports arena thrives on the practice of separating winners from losers, but no sports teams can survive without collaboration. That's one reason why athletes are often held up as role models: they are competitors who understand teamwork. Teams collaborate with schools and companies to improve their communities. Some of their collaborative efforts inspire young fans to learn STEM skills.

The NBA's New Orleans Pelicans have partnered with local schools and organizations in the Mississippi Delta to create STEMFEST and other STEM-related programs. In 2020, as everyone adapted to COVID restrictions, the Pelicans teamed with Chevron, Learn Fresh, and other organizations to sponsor a workshop for elementary and middle school students called "Scoring with STEM."[94] In real classrooms, socially distancing students were given the basic materials and challenged to build model basketball courts with tiny balls, baskets, and even buzzers. One participant streamed the event, showing teachers and students nationwide how this kind of engagement can bring collaboration within a competitive context.

At the second "Scoring with STEM" event in June 2021, STEM NOLA, a nonprofit providing STEM education services, partnered with the Pelicans and other companies and organizations "to offer students a fun and unique STEM experience, 'Scoring with STEM: Using the Game of Basketball to Learn STEM.'" According to the *Red Lake Nation News*, this event employed the time-honored method of teaching kids math and science through a popular sport.[95] Sports stats are one of the best ways to introduce young students to more complex mathematical processes.

These weren't the first STEM-supporting collaborations between the Pelicans and other participants, nor will they be the last. Team members and the Pelican mascot often visit New Orleans classrooms, encouraging young fans to enter the NBA's Math Hoops program. Math

---

94   Dodson, "New Orleans Pelicans."

95   *Red Lake Nation News*, "STEM NOLA."

Hoops pushes kids to learn math skills by compiling and analyzing sports statistics. It also provides course materials and STEM education training for over two hundred teachers in three Southern states.[96]

The numbers that grow out of professional sports have always been an avenue into math for younger students. At one time, these numbers were the province of little boys with baseball cards, where each player's most basic statistics were printed on the opposite side of the card. The boys had to learn enough math to make sense of the numbers. But the influence of statistics soon spread beyond baseball, and eventually women's sports got more attention. Now girls keep track of their favorite basketball players, golfers, and tennis stars, matching boys number for number. This automatically includes them in these sports-education collaborations.

NFL AND STEM RUNNING TOWARD THE END ZONE

Another great example of a STEM collaboration using sports statistics is the NFL Hall of Fame's Educational Outreach Program. In this program, the NFL Hall of Fame joins with schools to create programs where students learn math through analysis of pro football statistics. Like real coaches, they crunch the numbers and analyze their meaning.[97]

As Jacqueline Brannon Giles, professor of mathematics at Houston Community College, writes, "Millions of people are uplifted and inspired by great plays and touchdowns in mammoth football

---

96   Dodson, "New Orleans Pelicans."

97   Wells, "Fantastic NFL Data."

fields packed with millions of spectators. Why not embrace a vision that more students (perhaps millions) will get excited about using real-world data from those fantastic plays in football, and, metaphorically, run, run, run toward the end zone of excellence in learning and applying mathematics in the real world. The goal then is to get that touchdown and victory in mathematics and mathematics education in the United States of America."

Giles has joined with the NFL Hall and the National Association of Mathematicians to spark minority students' interest in math by introducing them to the numbers involved in football. In a call to action, her colleague Lieutenant Colonel Daniel Outing writes, "Reports indicate that students with a strong grasp of mathematics have an advantage in academics and in the job market regardless of ethnic background or family income.... With fewer minority high school students enrolling in rigorous mathematics courses, the pool of fully qualified minority college applicants is small. Consequently, the pool of potential mathematicians, scientists, and engineers is even smaller, [creating] an urgent need to intervene to encourage middle school students to continue studying mathematics in high school. Programs that inspire undergraduate mathematics students to continue studying mathematics in graduate school have already proven successful, e.g., SUMSRI at Miami University and SPIRAL at the University of Maryland. Similar programs developed for middle school students could increase the numbers of students taking rigorous mathematics courses in high school."[98]

These ventures are based on the premise that collaboration is a basic aspect of STEM from beginning to end. Efforts start with collaboration between schools, companies, and organizations; parents and teachers collaborate to adapt programs to the needs of their schools;

---

98   Wells.

students collaborate with each other to complete STEM projects. These cooperative efforts go far beyond sports.

NASA AND THE ART OF STEM STORYTELLING

One obvious form of collaboration can be seen in the joint efforts of government health, technology, and science agencies teaming with our nation's schools, research hospitals, and other learning institutions. This often comes with help from the private sector for research, testing, and development of new tools, products, and processes. NASA's Misti Moore has specialized in fostering this kind of creative collaboration.

One of the projects she promoted took an unusual approach to learning about STEM subjects, as NASA partnered with the University of Texas at El Paso (UTEP) in a $500,000 collaboration that applied the art of storytelling to the process of learning about complex technical subjects.[99]

UTEP's Nate Robinson, who served as team leader, told an interviewer, "Very few science, technology, engineering and math (STEM) programs engage learners through the contexts of stories, particularly from topic to topic through a cohesive and connected narrative. This proposal changes that through the use of an interdisciplinary team that creates stories driving interactive, inquiry-based learning through multimedia narratives."

Stories attract our interest. In a story, we see potential, then choice, then change. Things happen, and those events affect people. People are at the heart of any story.

---

99 UTEP News Archive, "UTEP Secures $500K."

A good story draws in its listeners until they become a part of that heart. Nate Robinson's team had their own ongoing story, and he expressed his fellow team members' feelings about NASA's help in moving that story forward: "As a team, we're really excited to see a vision we've shared and been developing for years receive funding and traction, and how much more so that it's from a world-renowned leader in innovation, NASA. We're also excited and honored that this model can be used nationally but is largely comprised of local talent— from the creative writer to the artist to the curriculum specialist."[100]

For Misti Moore and NASA, this was one more opportunity to encourage STEM learning. She's promoted STEM, STEM diversity, and STEM inclusion in a variety of collaborations between NASA, schools, and the private sector. In addition to UTEP, in 2015 she brought together NASA, Houston students, and the NBA's Houston Rockets for a "Rocket Science Launch Day" where young people could question NASA scientists.

She was also instrumental in collaborations involving NASA's Student Opportunities in Airborne Research (SOAR) missions, including one funding STEM doctoral students at Texas Southern University. At this writing, she is running NASA's MUREP Innovation Tech Transfer Idea Competition (MITTIC).[101]

As Ms. Moore has said, she tries to create collaborations where "the work students are doing at their institution also meets with the work that is happening here related to NASA's mission. It shows the students that the work they do is very relevant and will be useful once they graduate."

---

100 UTEP News Archive.

101 Moore, "MUREP."

STEM AND SUSTAINABILITY ON THE HAWAIIAN ISLANDS

Another good example of a STEM collaboration involving students emerged to meet a real-world challenge: the need for sustainable, locally produced energy on the islands of Hawaii.

One Hawaiian middle school student expressed the project's problem this way: "What if a tsunami hits Hawaii and cuts off our fossil fuel energy supply?" Students imagined their homes without running water or even electric lights.[102]

This Hawaiian STEM project is named Ka Hei. The name comes from a particular kind of snare made by looping and knotting rope. Hawaiian tradition holds that the Hawaiian god Maui used a Ka Hei to capture the sun, and the phrase has come to mean "to absorb knowledge or skill."

Ka Hei is a collaboration between Hawaii's Department of Education (DOE), OpTerra Energy Services, and other private companies. The Hawaiian DOE's website states, "As a comprehensive energy and sustainability program, Ka Hei will transform the learning environment, reduce operational expenses and provide engaging educational opportunities for our students and community."

Reporter Tara Smith wrote at techlearning.com, "Whether you call it STEM, STEAM, or STREAM, cross-curricular, real-world education is helping students to make a difference in their communities…. And creative collaboration is the key."

Smith quotes Brent Suyama of Hawaii DOE, who describes Ka Hei as "a multipronged approach to sustainability and incorporation of STEM." Smith tells her readers that even the name is collabora-

---

102 Smith, "Collaboration."

tive. It involves a Hawaiian god who employs a kind of engineered technology, using knowledge and skills he's absorbed—a collaboration of concept, learning, and action.

The problem presented to Hawaii's students was to create a sustainable energy system for that state's schools, one that wouldn't be dependent on imported fossil fuel—a system that could withstand a hypothetical tsunami. The biggest challenge was the fact that Hawaii is made up of islands two thousand miles from the West Coast. That meant as many energy sources as possible had to be local to Hawaii. The emphasis would be on renewable energy. In its search for solutions, Ka Hei operated on what Smith called "the three *Es*— efficiency, electricity generation, and education."[103]

The program began with energy audits of Hawaii's public schools—all 256 of them. Students collaborated to identify problems and solve them. Some fixes were easy and only involved equipment, such as switching to more energy-efficient LED light bulbs. Others required more collaborative actions from all stakeholders. These included turning off lights and faucets, reporting and fixing leaks, and educating students and staff about energy and water conservation.

The motivation to find solutions was strong. The communities use many of these schools as emergency shelters during hurricanes and other natural cataclysms, so the schools need secure energy systems that won't fail, even when larger systems do.

This is a case where collaboration goes together with competition. For instance, students joined together in teams and collaborated on a project to identify their most wasteful energy habits. Each team examined its own class members to see what behaviors were most wasteful and how students could alter those behaviors. The teams added up the energy savings, then calculated the costs.

---

103 Smith.

The team that created the most savings at the least cost won and got credit for their accomplishment. That's the competition. But when this energy-saving program is put into practice, all the school's students participate, collaborate, and reap the benefits.

In the Ka Hei program, changes in behavior are matched by advances in energy-saving engineering and technology. As Smith writes, "Ka Hei is taking advantage of the sun and wind, exploring innovative energy technology, and installing photovoltaic (PV) panels. Eighty schools benefited from a narrow window offering net energy agreements, and efforts to find creative ways to finance PV panels for the rest of the schools and to establish microgrids in five pilot schools are ongoing. This next phase, with the ultimate goal of net-zero buildings, also involves engineering storage solutions."[104]

COLLABORATION IN CLASSROOMS

Energy is an obvious STEM-related area where students can collaborate on projects that create real change that they can see and measure. Another recent real-world STEM-related problem has been that of getting kids back into classrooms. As of this writing, many students have finally resumed normal classes. As this has happened, most parents, kids, and teachers are glad to see schools open again.

In Indianapolis, when students began returning to Sunny Heights Elementary School in July 2021, one STEM teacher, Kelsey Walters, exulted, "I'm so excited to have them back."[105] Walters began with the

---

104 Smith.

105 Pointer, "Teachers, Staff Prep."

problems left by lingering COVID protocols. "So, I had to figure out where I want everything to be, how do I want the kids to sit. Which is again another challenge with everything that's going on," she said.

Indianapolis school superintendent Dr. Tim Hanson described a process where collaboration is key, and solutions follow the science. Hanson worked with all stakeholders, reviewing the latest postings from all pertinent authorities, from the CDC to the County Public Health Department. "As you know, COVID is ever changing," Dr. Hanson told a reporter. "Unfortunately, right now [July 28, 2021], our COVID data in Marion County is trending up.... Hopefully that reverses and goes the other direction, and we'll re-evaluate where we are and potentially, we can be either removing restrictions, keeping them the same or worst-case scenario increasing them."[106]

This flexible attitude is necessary as more and more students are returning amid fluctuations in COVID rates. Teachers like Walters are glad to see the kids, and they are adapting to new situations day by day. "As a STEM teacher, there's a lot of collaboration," says Walters. "Also what's going to work best for the classroom. To have them be able to get their hands on a project, work together, share ideas with each other, and then see the same final product, you can't do that virtually."

With schools finally open, educators and parents all over the country are facing similar problems. On the one hand, we all want to return to normal as fast as we possibly can. On the other hand, we've learned about the need for making learning environments safe. That means we must weigh the social benefits of a return to real classrooms against scientific concerns about the virus, expressed in cold hard math. At this writing, that math is improving, but schools still face uncertainty about the future.

---

106 Pointer.

Like other school officials from Maine to California, those in Indianapolis are puzzling over the science, technology, and engineering of various solutions. One school system puts a container of hand sanitizer in every locker, while another requires masks, even outdoors. Some will continue with remote learning, but all look forward to a day when classrooms are normal again.

PANDEMIC IMPACTS ON STEM

Like every other part of education, STEM programs have suffered in the pandemic. Students, like those in Kelsey Walters's classes, had to close STEM projects or put them on hold. In September 2020, when schools were adapting to the prospect of a school year without classrooms, Madeleine Gregory wrote in the Sierra Club's online magazine, "One type of class is particularly difficult to move online: lab classes. Many courses in the STEM fields … include lab or field classes as practical components to an otherwise theoretical course."[107]

> *Like every other part of education, STEM programs have suffered in the pandemic.*

Professors are now tasked with converting this experiential learning—which relies on the student's ability to touch and see and feel the lesson—to a flat, remote interface.… COVID-19 threatens to change the meaning of a STEM degree. Can a student graduate in biology having never learned to perform fundamental pro-

---

107 Gregory, "How the Pandemic."

cedures? Can they graduate in forestry if they've never done fieldwork in an actual forest? We're about to find out."

In 2020–2021, our schools survived more than a year without classrooms—or labs—and now teachers are scrambling to assess and repair whatever damage might have been done to real learning. Much of this work is STEM-related, and that always involves collaboration.

STEM RECOVERY PROGRAMS

In another Indiana-based project, the state government has awarded Indiana University $4.4 million from the Student Learning Recovery Grant program.[108] The university's faculty members have collaborated to create several projects with these funds, including the following:

- "Project Lift" has $690,000 available to bring STEM literacy and STEM education together, so students in K–8 can collaborate on projects with titles like "Readable English" and "Novel Engineering."

- A grant of $567,640 to the university's School of Education for "Girls STEM Institute: Advancing Learning through Interdisciplinary Experiences." According to an Indiana University press release, this institute "is designed to provide holistic learning opportunities for Girls of Color, who have been historically marginalized in STEM fields, and provide a support system focused on their STEM identity and overall well-being."

---

108 Whitaker, "State Awards IU."

■ A $672,000 fund for IU's Kokomo School of Education, which is working with two Howard County school districts to combat COVID learning losses.

As we can see from these projects, virtually all STEM education relies on collaboration. With COVID, this has become even more clear. When students form teams and divide tasks, they learn how collaboration works and what it can achieve.

STEM teachers know the value of this, and right now they're collaborating with parents and other stakeholders to bring students back together in the same classrooms and labs. School administrators are collaborating with parents and business owners to design programs that will bridge the gap and retrieve the essential learning these students lacked for a year and a half.

The collaboration required by STEM projects is now necessary in the biggest STEM project of all: the redemption of America's schools as they reemerge from their COVID cocoon.

CHAPTER 8

ACCESS!
SPREADING
THE WORD FOR
BROADBAND

From teachforamerica.org:

> At Leslie County High School, an expansive brick building backdropped by the rolling hills of Eastern Kentucky, Lydia Weiso's AP English students were deep in discussion about their strategies for getting work done online.

> Jaden travels to the school where his mom works to upload files for his college credit work. Jasmine goes up on the

mountain near her house. Above the trees, she gets the clear cell service she needs to do her homework ...

Without access to high-speed broadband internet at home, students like Jaden and Jasmine—not to mention teachers like Lydia—are forced to find clever solutions like these to get their assignments done and stay connected. "As teachers, we're always looking for everyday workarounds," says Lydia, who moved to Leslie County in 2018 to join Teach For America. "What can I just print and go? What can I alter? How can I show this video?"[109]

What Ms. Weiso, Jaden, and Jasmine need is better access to broadband. What's become standard for many of us is still out of reach for kids in their school.

When your parents were growing up, no one had heard of "broadband." The internet was something that existed in a few computer labs. Education was available in schools, classrooms, libraries, and books. It also might have involved photos, films, and audio recordings, but most learning—the kind that earned degrees and certifications—was done the old way: listening to teachers or studying textbooks.

When personal computers became common in America's homes, the internet followed almost immediately. As the online world grew, it soaked up the knowledge from all human history, while adding incredible troves of new data every day, not all of it reliable. Twenty years ago, the internet started spreading from our desktops, jumping to our laptops, tablets, and phones, then taking over our TVs and radios. It crept into our cars, telling us where to go, and then it spread

---

109 Fregni, "How Rural Students."

out to our traffic lights and security cameras. For good or for ill, the online world has permeated the bricks-and-mortar world, and in many ways, they are now one and the same.

Many of us recall dial-up access to the internet. This once seemed like a miracle, but it was quickly eclipsed by DSL (a digital subscriber line). DSL still received information through the phone lines, but it could break down and reorganize data to speed up the transmission. This meant users received more information in shorter time spans. This was fine for our desktop computers, but as our devices became portable, we needed more and more speed and storage. The cloud solved the storage problem, but moving information around required a broad mix of communications technologies. This is what we now define as *broadband.*

Broadband is becoming our present, and it will rule our future. That future will depend on the STEM skills of students who are in our schools now. Many of these students are females and Children of Color. These are the ones who need the best STEM training we can give them. They are our future. Broadband is their lifeline to a better world. According to the National Telecommunications and Information Administration (NTIA), "Maximizing broadband coverage and meaningful use is an imperative for national and individual success."[110]

BROADBAND AS A GATEWAY TO STEM

Access to broadband internet increases a student's potential to successfully navigate through the worlds of commerce, education, govern-

---

110   BroadbandUSA, "What Is NTIA?"

ment, health, sports, and virtually any other field. Building the world of broadband requires STEM skills. Increasingly, broadband internet is the best gateway to learning these skills.

Broadband is a basic component in our nation's infrastructure. In the last two years, Americans have been more and more concerned with infrastructure. It's been the subject of a massive new law, which focused the national debate on infrastructure issues. What is *infrastructure*? It's the foundation and framework of our modern lives. Most people agree that America's infrastructure needs work. We cross crumbling bridges, drive down potholed roads, and know that we must build a truly modern transportation system.

What we don't see as clearly is the fact that today's transportation systems require more than concrete, asphalt, and guardrails. Today's highways, railroads, and planes need communications infrastructure. Individuals need interconnected communications for everything from GPS systems to the operation of driverless cars. Cities need information from speed cameras, car counters, and traffic signals. All of this is as basic to modern infrastructure as traffic lights and road signs.

A 2021 law governing the expansion and renewal of America's infrastructure appropriates $65 billion over the next ten years to increase access to broadband. This investment recognizes the nation's future needs, but it must also address the access issues of our underserved communities. A recent post on route-fifty.com reported on the findings of a Brookings Institution study:

> Ensuring prospective workers beginning their careers remains a challenge, especially for women and People of Color who are underrepresented across these jobs according to Brooking research.

The lack of gender and racial diversity results from several factors: a lack of visibility and community engagement; limited supportive services, including childcare and transportation access; and a lack of employer flexibility and resources to help nontraditional individuals navigate unwelcoming workplaces.

Regional leaders should view their infrastructure workforce needs in light of the needs of their entire community in line with strategies emerging nationally around a more equitable post-COVID economy, the organization says.[111]

America's girls and Children of Color need access to broadband so that they can learn the kinds of STEM skills that make broadband happen. Many of these skills are dependent on the speed and breadth of broadband. Now, these young people are still woefully underrepresented in STEM occupations.

An article on zdnet.com reports that "Since 1990, STEM employment has increased by almost 80%, from 9.7 million to 17.3 million STEM jobs. While women comprise 47% of all workers in the U.S., they represent only 24% of the STEM workforce."[112]

Even this 24% figure is misleading. Women aren't evenly spread out across STEM disciplines. They are the vast majority of our healthcare providers, holding about three out of four healthcare jobs, but according to the zdnet.com story, "There is still a shortage of women in other STEM careers, including engineering, computer, and physics."

---

111   Route Fifty, "Broadband."

112   Reviews.com Staff, "Bridging the Gender Divide."

RURAL SCHOOLS OFTEN LEFT BEHIND

Why are girls and Children of Color still underrepresented in STEM classrooms? The one in six students in our rural schools face unique obstacles in STEM. Rural areas have a hard time attracting math and science teachers, and the teachers they do get don't stick around. Also, many of the programs aimed at expanding STEM access are geared toward urban schools.

As the zdnet.com article reports, "[Rural schools] also do not always have access to high-quality STEM learning opportunities that other schools have, which leaves their students behind in both exposure and education. Pair this lack of access with the barriers young girls feel about their abilities in the subjects, and you see a detrimental pattern forming."[113]

There's also the centuries-long tradition of favoring boys. It's so ingrained that even now we often have a hard time recognizing it. As Girl Scouts of the USA CEO Sylvia Acevedo has observed, "A girl who tries a STEM assignment or activity and doesn't do well the first time maybe makes an assumption that she's not good at it because she's a girl rather than because of how the subject is being introduced or taught to her."[114]

Broadband increases access, and when students gain access, this gives them more opportunities. When young people are presented with opportunities, they often need mentors to advise and guide them. These mentors play a big role. They help students take advantage of these broadband opportunities, steering them to sites where they will

---

113 Reviews.com Staff.

114 Editors, "Role of Girl Scouts."

find real treasure. It's essential for students to have role models, so the best mentors are women and People of Color who have mastered the basics of the broadband metaverse.

The Smithsonian Science Education Center's Dr. Carol O'Donnell has promoted the idea of a "STEM education ecosystem."[115] This is the whole environment of the STEM student: school, home, and community. It's e-books, websites, libraries, research institutions, and any other sources of STEM information. When a young student wades into this sea of information, a good mentor is invaluable.

A mentor can help a young Girl of Color feel as if she belongs in this world. A mentor can help her take advantage of broadband's advantages. A good mentor can help a young girl raise her self-esteem. Once she believes in herself, a girl can imagine the woman she wants to become and aim for that goal. This can lead her into new adventures in learning and discovery.

Dr. O'Donnell's personal experience motivates her crusade for STEM mentorship. She knew from the start that she wanted to work in science, but the only role models she had were her science teachers. So, she started out to become a science teacher. Today she says, "That was all I really thought I was capable of. Looking back, I wish that I had more opportunities for female role models who were in engineers' or scientists' positions."

As the fastest-growing sector in the online world, broadband can be a great new opportunity for STEM students of all backgrounds. This is the moment when girls and Children of Color can stake their claim to their fair share of the future. We must help all of them do that so that they can reach for the stars.

---

115   Smithsonian Institute, "Carol O'Donnell."

CHAPTER 9

TOMORROW!

BUILDING THE
BEST FUTURE

Wikipedia tells us that "patient capital" is another name for funds invested for long-term benefits.[116] This is different from short-term investments, where investors want to make money immediately, or at least very soon. If a short-term investment can't produce profits in a year or two, these financial backers lose interest. When they invest in a project, they intend their investment to be short-term capital, but some ventures require more time and vision. That's when patient capital comes in.

Patient capital is a term that nearly describes itself. It refers to money invested for the future, and it's often meant to produce benefits

116   Wikimedia Foundation, "Patient Capital."

that won't be seen for many years. With patient capital, the investor is willing to make a financial investment in a business or enterprise, usually with no expectation of getting any quick return whatsoever. As the Wikipedia author explains, "Instead, the investor is willing to forgo an immediate return in anticipation of more substantial returns down the road."

The Wikipedia author cites pension funds, university endowments, and sovereign wealth funds as examples of this kind of capital.

> *Patient capital ... refers to money invested for the future, and it's often meant to produce benefits that won't be seen for many years.*

When a young worker pays into her pension fund, she knows she won't see profits for several decades. The money is meant to finance her retirement. When a wealthy philanthropist donates millions to a school's endowment, he may not expect any return in his lifetime. The benefits from his patient capital investment will emerge in hundreds or even thousands of college educations.[117]

Many of the students he's investing in haven't been born yet. When a government establishes a sovereign wealth fund (SWF) to invest in a struggling new industry, no one anticipates profits for years, or perhaps not even until the next generation. These kinds of investors, institutions, and investments rely on security and long-term benefits. That's why "patient capital" has often been referred to as "long-term capital."

---

117 Wikimedia Foundation.

There's a lot in a name. "Long-term capital" sounds like a pool of cash, sitting undisturbed, waiting to be spent. "Patient capital" sounds more like money that's already out there, gradually working through a slow but steady process toward a defined goal. We knew the goal when we invested our money; our investment creates funds for purchasing, hiring, and other actions, while we patiently await the results.

One of the longest-running examples of a patient capital investment is the basic US savings bond. This investment can cost as little as fifty dollars and accrues interest for twenty years. The investor is putting his faith in the continued operations of the federal government. Government bonds don't pay the highest interest, but most buyers appreciate the security of government guarantees and the knowledge that their money is funding public improvements.

When we invest patient capital, we know our investment will help build laboratories, rent offices, fund research, and develop new products and services. It can also pay for public health initiatives, education, and transportation. These kinds of investments often rely on the provision of tax dollars. As with sovereign wealth funds, these are a public form of patient capital, and a lot of it goes into building and maintaining our roads and public schools.

We expect benefits from these investments, but we know we won't see some of the promised improvements for decades. A road or bridge will bring benefits as soon as it's opened, but it might take years to build, and decades must pass before we realize its full benefits. When children go to school, they are learning the skills they will need to do good work, but those skills aren't likely to bear fruit until the children grow up and get their first jobs.

The goal of patient capital is simple: to build a better future. We go into these investments accepting their long-term nature because we care about the future and the world we will leave to our children.

In that sense, "patient capital" is exactly what the words mean: *capital* invested with a *patient* approach.

PATIENT CAPITAL'S MOON SHOT

One of the most obvious examples of patient capital's effects in a STEM-related venture can be seen in the race to the moon. In early 1961, as John Kennedy's presidency was just beginning, America and Russia were competing in a race to achieve space firsts. The Russians had already launched successful satellites and probes, and they'd put the first man in space early that year. That's when Kennedy committed valuable American resources of time, talent, and dollars to land someone on the moon, then return that person safely to Earth. He challenged America to beat our Russian competitors and do this by 1970.

As the 1960s opened, this seemed like an impossibility for either country, but Kennedy saw it as an inspiring dream whose achievement could elevate America's sprit and make our people proud. Though Kennedy didn't live to see it, the nation reached the goal he'd set. Expressed in 2022 currency, the moon shot turned into a quarter-of-a-trillion-dollar journey ($250,000,000,000.00).[118] By the end of July 1969, five months ahead of schedule, two American astronauts had walked on the surface of another world. In the next three years, five more landings and ten more astronauts followed.

During the moon race, and in its immediate aftermath, many people questioned the value of this massive effort. In the end, their views prevailed. Since the last Apollo flight in 1972, no other human

---

118   Reichhardt, "To the Moon."

being has visited the moon. It provides us with no essential materials, and there are no immediate plans for colonization. Yet, if we are looking for a good return on our patient capital, few investments can match that of putting those twelve people on our nearest neighbor. NASA dedicates a page of its website to show just a few of the discoveries from the space race that have made our lives easier since then.

Guidance systems are now a basic part of our daily lives, but that wasn't true then. In 1969, TV viewers were amazed at the system that steered the lunar module to a safe landing among the boulders. Soon, similar systems were landing airliners, and today we have improved versions in the form of GPS guidance and the parking cameras in our cars.

These systems hold the imminent promise of self-driving cars. When NASA needed space-age insulation, it funded the development of Mylar. Today this amazing material is used in everything from T-shirts to desktop keyboards. Space-age requirements for food safety have led to safer food for all of us, and NASA's shock absorbers made earthbound buildings more earthquake-proof. Advances that went into the moon landings have helped us do everything from building highways to raising crops, yet today some think the program that produced these miracles was a waste of time, effort, and money.[119]

President Kennedy knew better. Though he realized many of the space program's technological breakthroughs wouldn't bring real benefits until the distant future, he was ready to risk the capital and to be patient. In a 1962 speech answering the space program's critics, he said, "We choose to go to the moon in this decade and do the other things, not because they are easy, but because they are hard, because that goal will serve to organize and measure the best of our energies

---

119 Hall, "Going to the Moon."

and skills, because that challenge is one that we are willing to accept, one we are unwilling to postpone, and one which we intend to win."

JFK began our nation's investment of this tranche of patient capital in 1961. A generation later, in 1990, the first President Bush said the money we had spent to get to the moon was "the best return on investment since Leonardo da Vinci bought himself a sketchpad." One NASA administrator at the time, Admiral Richard Truly, was willing to put this return in dollar figures, saying that "a payback of $7 or 8 for every $1 invested over a period of a decade, or so has been calculated, for the Apollo Program."[120]

Truly also noted the program's positive impact on education and technological development, especially considering that even at its peak in the late 1960s, it took up only 4% of the federal budget. A NASA study done almost forty years after the start of our nation's space program showed that with technology transfer and spin-off industries, every dollar spent on space research generated forty dollars worth of economic growth on Earth. How many other ventures can make such claims? Very few, if any. That's the power of patient capital when we invest it in STEM fields like space travel.[121]

HIDDEN FIGURES CELEBRATED

We have already cited some of the unsung STEM heroes of the space race whose mathematical skills kept the astronauts on course. These heroes—Women of Color—were finally honored and celebrated

---

120 Globus, "Optimum Financing."

121 Globus.

in the movie *Hidden Figures*.[122] Their salaries, labs, and equipment were financed by our nation's patient capital, and that investment has been paying us back ever since. First it paid off in a successful space program, but the work of the people on the ground also led to better digital tools, programs, software, and hardware. These inventions made the internet possible, as well as smartphones and many other wonders of modern communications.

The women in *Hidden Figures* had many sisters doing similar work, but few observers noticed at the time. Their stories were obscured then, but now these STEM pioneers are being honored. One program that honors them, through education of today's youth, is transportation and technology expert William "Bill" Montgomery's Hidden Pioneers.[123] Montgomery works with NASA, educators, and students to encourage today's young trailblazers to study, learn, and make their marks. He brings NASA to our nation's schools, and he welcomes students to NASA, helping young People of Color find their unique roles in the world of science, technology, engineering, and math—the skills NASA needs.

Montgomery commented on one personal effect of this cycle of learning in an interview with eshemagazine.com at the 2nd Annual Global Diversity Summit: "It was about three years ago when I found out that my cousin [Katherine Johnson, who was portrayed in the film] worked for NASA, and she helped us get to the moon and back safely. I was interested and did my R&D to find some amazing people that want to help my mission. I'm still working with them today.... NASA is great; they are all about the TEAM. We are blessed from the beginning till the end, why not help each other and love daily?"[124]

---

122 Shetterly, "Hidden Figures."

123 Jordan, "William Montgomery."

124 Jordan.

As we can see from all these stories, patient wealth is a long-term process that helps us pass financial and educational advantages from one generation to the next. Established companies spend patient capital on research and development. States, counties, and cities sell government bonds for everything from schools to stadiums. When individual investors like us buy these kinds of bonds, we are adding to the pool of patient capital and investing in the future.

ALL HIGHWAYS LEAD TO PATIENT CAPITAL

So, beyond individual bond buyers, where does all the other patient capital come from? As we mentioned before, it has both public and private sources. Governments often furnish it, especially in enterprises with costs beyond the reach of any private individual or combination.

Our government's most famous investment in this kind of patient capital is expenditures for our forty-seven-thousand-mile system of interstate highways. The cost of building the system was roughly half a trillion dollars (as measured in 2016 dollars).[125] So far, our return on that investment is somewhere between $3 trillion and $4 trillion, or about six to eight dollars for each dollar invested—not so different from Admiral Truly's estimate of return from our investment in the space race.

Both ventures needed a lot of patient capital, far more than private industry or individuals could invest. They were national efforts that had enough support from taxpayers to go forward. That's why NASA was the primary driver of America's space effort in the twentieth

---

125 Hale, "Happy Birthday, Interstate."

century; only the national government had access to enough money. By the early twenty-first century, the effort was up and running. That's when billionaire investors began to play a role in space travel. Where would they be today without the patient capital investments of the past?

Private individuals and companies invest patient capital only when their long-range interests are matched by current, sustainable profits. For instance, today's largest communications companies use current profits to invest in cycles of communications satellite systems.

These satellites are expensive to design, build, and launch, but they don't cost much to maintain. A satellite that wears out can be replaced. A well-designed communications satellite system might take five years to design and five years to complete, and then it might last for fifteen years or more up in orbit. When a company invests in such a system, it knows it won't see returns for several years. That's a good example of private patient capital.

PATIENT CAPITAL AND FUTURE STEM

How does patient capital figure into the STEM equation? One example is easy to follow: Investments in STEM education for preschoolers won't produce real financial value for many years, yet these investments are essential allocations of our capital, public and private. Those preschoolers are the doctors, researchers, and rocket scientists of 2050. If we don't invest patient capital in their early education, our nation's efforts in STEM areas could be derailed. Those areas include everything from food production to entertainment to the latest iteration of online tools.

One international healthcare company that understands this equation is pharmaceutical giant GlaxoSmithKline (GSK), which has its United States headquarters in Philadelphia. In February 2021, GSK announced support for two new programs aimed at providing "equitable STEM education across schools in Philadelphia," according to one company press release.[126] One area requiring funding during the pandemic: digital-learning platforms.

Philadelphia schools have been dependent on these platforms throughout the shutdown. According to its press release, GSK is spending more than $100,000 on one solution: "online science lab software for K–12 students so that they may engage in inquiry-based science learning from home." These platforms are helping young people learn new STEM skills even during the pandemic. According to GSK, the funds "will also support ongoing equitable science instruction once students return to school buildings, ensuring that students in all grade levels can conduct scientific experiments even if lab space and materials are limited."

Philadelphia District teachers can also apply for mini grants from this program "to develop hands-on STEM activities for students." In addition, there are funds for virtual labs where students can share in discoveries that "provide more opportunities to spark creativity and imagination with our students," according to elementary school science teacher Tienne Myers.[127]

The fact that this funding goes to a large city's public school system guarantees that it will benefit underserved children. Additionally, 85% of Philadelphia's public school students are Black, and other

---

126 Berland, "GSK Announces over $1M."

127 Berland.

minority students are also enrolled. GSK is targeting all underserved students. It supports "a $500,000, two-year pilot training program for 100 [Philadelphia] District middle school math and science teachers to implement new curricula and increase participation, engagement, and success for girls and Students of Color."

The company's gift will fund grants for STEM enrichment and internship programs targeting girls, women, and Black and Latinx students. Other beneficiaries include a College of Physicians STEM Internship Program, linking STEM learning with social justice, and the Philadelphia Robotics Coalition, supporting robotics clubs in Philadelphia public schools. (After all, what STEM-inclined kid doesn't like robots?)

GSK's website tells readers that "these grants build on the work of the Philadelphia STEM Equity Collective, a city-wide, collaborative effort launched by GSK and the Philadelphia Education Fund in 2020. GSK has committed to invest $10 million over 10 years to support this effort.… GSK is also contributing the time and talent of GSK volunteers to staff the Philadelphia STEM Equity Collective." With its solid foundation in this Equity Collective and its full decade of funding, this is a classic example of the use of private patient capital to advance a public cause.

Becki Lynch, director of US community partnerships at GSK, expressed the company's reasons this way: "We are proud of our long history at GSK of investing philanthropic dollars in STEM education programs in the Philadelphia region, especially those focused on increasing access and improving outcomes for students who are under-represented in STEM careers."[128]

---

128 Berland.

IMPACT INVESTING

Sometimes investments of patient capital are also investments of venture capital, where the financial backing takes the traditional form of stock or bond purchases. This often happens when a company is just getting started. Investors see a good idea, but one that isn't likely to pay off for many years. They know that a dollar invested now might produce hundreds of dollars a generation from now. These investors are looking for places to put their patient capital, but they allow their prejudices—conscious and unconscious—to rule their choices.

Those choices often exclude women and minorities, and that exclusion can stop a new technology in its tracks. "Entrepreneurs who are marginalized represent missed opportunities to bring promising new technologies to the market," the national president of the Association for Women in Science (AWIS), Susan Windham-Bannister, said recently. "We strongly encourage investors and funders to broaden their scope of interest and expand their investment portfolios to include highly capable entrepreneurs who are women, racially and ethnically diverse and often overlooked and excluded from access to capital."[129]

One answer to this is a form of private patient capital known as "impact investing." According to a recent article by Lucy Wilson on the start-up news website beauhurst.com, "In recent years, patient capital has also come to be associated with impact investing. In this context, rather than maximizing immediate returns for shareholders, the focus is on maximizing the positive social or environmental impact of an investment, alongside financial gains. Nonprofit investment fund Acumen, for instance, defines patient capital as 'investment in an early-stage enterprise providing low-income consumers

---

129 Ibañez, "AWIS Calls on VCs."

with access to healthcare, water, housing, alternative energy, or agricultural inputs.'"[130]

Acumen's website introduces itself with this description of their approach to these investments: "Patient capital investing bridges the gap between the efficiency and scale of market-based approaches and the social impact of pure philanthropy. Patient capital has a high tolerance for risk, has long time horizons, is flexible to meet the needs of entrepreneurs, and is unwilling to sacrifice the needs of end customers for the sake of shareholders. At the same time, patient capital ultimately demands accountability in the form of a return on capital: proof that the underlying enterprise can grow sustainably in the long run."[131]

This kind of patient capital relies mainly on private investors who want a better world along with a long-term return on their money.

FUNDING IMPACT
IN THE CLOUD

Another private company that's not afraid to invest patient capital is the Boston-based cloud-storage provider Carbonite.[132] Its website describes Carbonite Inc. as a "robust Data Protection Platform for businesses, including backup, disaster recovery, high availability, and workload migration technology. The Carbonite Data Protection Platform supports businesses on a global scale with secure Cloud infrastructure." That means their business isn't just *in* the cloud, it *is*

---

130   Wilson, "Understanding Patient Capital."

131   Acumen, "Patient Capital."

132   Carbonite, "About Carbonite."

the cloud. They operate in that world, making their part of the cloud secure and civilized so the rest of us can store our data safely and get a good night's sleep.

Like the cloud itself, Carbonite is young. The company only came into existence in 2006. It was one of the earliest pioneers in commercial digital storage. The company's founders recognized the cloud's potential, clearly seeing its increasing role in data storage. It began by hiring technicians who had the most up-to-date skills of that era, and for fifteen years it has continued to develop workforce skills that always stay a step ahead of the competition. When OpenText bought Carbonite in 2019, this process barely missed a beat. Carbonite retained its identity, continued the business of secure data storage, and kept up its philanthropic efforts.

When a company's business is completely in the cloud, that company is going to have to hire workers whose skills are on STEM's cutting edge. In today's increasingly digital world, these kinds of STEM workers are beginning their training as far back as the cradle, where they might be found shaking computerized baby rattles. Those rattles, and more advanced pre-K STEM programs, require investment of patient capital in early education.

Though the future often looks murky, this is the kind of private investment a digital company must make. Without these funds, there might not be any digital companies in our future, but once the investments are made, the coming decades look bright!

Carbonite's vehicle for investment in the future has been the Carbonite Charitable Fund.[133] From its recent creation in 2018, this proactive nonprofit has provided students with STEM training. Concentrating their efforts in New England and the Boston area, Carbonite Charitable Fund has also funded STEM programs in other

---

133 Carbonite, "Carbonite Charitable Fund."

parts of the country. As one Carbonite spokesman said on the eve of the company's sale to OpenText, "The organizations we support commit to improving STEM learning experiences and continue to demonstrate meaningful results.... Carbonite's grant recipients are actively involved in finding ways for all students to interact with STEM. We look forward to our ongoing partnership with the leading organizations that are preparing the next generation for their technology careers."

This has led Carbonite and its buyer to give STEM education grants to efforts like Hack.Diversity. Hack.Diversity has been described on a Boston STEM website as a "regional initiative from the New England Venture Capital Association to increase the number of Black and Latino employees in the innovation economy in Boston by 100%."[134] Another recipient of a Carbonite grant is Resilient Coders, "a regional program in Boston that trains People of Color for high growth careers as software engineers and connects them with technology jobs."[135] Carbonite's patient capital has also funded early STEM education efforts in other states, including Indiana and Utah.

> *Traditionally marginalized groups will soon be a majority. That means their need for current STEM training is greater than ever.*

Carbonite, OpenText, GSK, and other like-minded companies and their subsidiaries understand the need for investments of patient capital in STEM programs. They are led by STEM-educated entrepre-

---

134   NEVCA, "Hack.Diversity."

135   Engel, "Resilient Coders."

neurs who put faith in their skills and have used those skills to build companies. These companies realize they will need many more people with STEM training if they're going to earn profits.

Some of the children who benefit from these investments will eventually work for these companies, but STEM training is also vital to each company's clients. They know that their white-dominated culture is opening to a world filled with minorities, women, and People of Color. When we look at US census projections, it's clear that these traditionally marginalized groups will soon be a majority. That means their need for current STEM training is greater than ever. The best place to start and have the greatest impact is during a child's earliest learning. This is when all our investments are long-term.

The most likely sources of private patient capital are companies like GSK and Carbonite—businesses built on (and dependent on) a foundation of evolving technology. To them, patient capital is very similar to venture capital: money invested in a far-off future when new inventions and methods multiply every dollar. As Christine Hockley, director of investments at British Patient Capital, has noted, "Venture capital is predominantly invested in tech-driven businesses that require STEM skills."[136]

That's why the leaders of these kinds of companies believe in patient capital. When they look at today's minority students, they are thinking about the long run. They know what to do from their own past experience as students. For a better tomorrow, they invest in the students of today.

---

136 Private Equity Wire, "Women in VC."

CHAPTER 10

REVELATION!

ONCE A SOLUTION EXISTS, THE PROBLEM DOESN'T

If we *can't* do something we need to do, that's a problem. If we *can* do it, we might never even know that the potential for a problem existed. So, once we solve a problem, the road ahead becomes clear.

Take the problem of climbing stairs in tall buildings. For thousands of years, a building couldn't be more than a few floors high. If they'd built them any higher, few people would have been willing to climb to the upper levels. Then Elisha Otis invented the safety elevator, and it wasn't long before New York had a whole skyline of tall buildings. The solution became such a basic part of urban architecture that few could recall the problem.

Another seemingly eternal problem was lighting the darkness at night. Darkness made even the shortest trips difficult, and those who ventured out after sunset risked injury, robbery, or getting lost, any one of which might end in death or damaged health. Candles were a weak fix, and though gas was much brighter, it was also dirty, dangerous, and difficult to deliver anywhere beyond central towns and inner cities.

As scientists uncovered the secrets of electricity, thousands of inventors competed to turn electric current into light. Thomas Edison stole a march on them all when he invented the light bulb. Within three years, his glowing bulbs were lighting a section of New York's streets. A few decades later, every major American city lit most of its streets at night. The problem of lighting the darkness had vanished from existence (though soon some astronomers began noticing the effects of light pollution in the night sky).

Once we invented an effective mousetrap, mice stopped troubling our thoughts. Once we solved the problem of fire, we could cook, stay warm, and have just enough light to get us by until that guy Edison came along. Each problem has a solution, and once we find that solution, the problem passes into nonexistence.

That's how it should work with the problems of equity, access, inclusion, and diversity in STEM education. The obstacles to equity in STEM classrooms are a problem. Students from disadvantaged homes start out with one strike against them. Those who face race, gender, or any other form of prejudice get a second strike called on them before they even enroll. That's a long way from equity. But if school administrators see this and help these kids with the best teachers and resources they can find, those strikes of prejudice will turn into academic home runs—problem solved.

Now our students have equity, but there's still the next problem: access. What if bigotry, financial difficulties, or geography limit a child's choice of schools, making the best STEM programs inaccessible? Educators and parents might join together to bring high-quality STEM programs to the child's neighborhood school, or they could identify the closest quality program that would provide transportation. With either solution, the child can forget about the problem and concentrate on his or her studies.

When the Child of Color finds a good school, that child might still be excluded from necessary STEM classes or activities. But if a good teacher sees this and rectifies the situation, allowing the child's intelligence to shine brightly, exclusion becomes inclusion, and there is no problem. And if this happens with every needy child, these solutions to problems in equity, access, and inclusion will also render problems in diversity nonexistent.

At its best, STEM education is an adventure in problem-solving. Our teacher might ask us to design a way to get to Mars. She holds out Mars as the solution to the problem of where humans will go when Earth is too crowded. Or the STEM problem might be locating a new reservoir so that it collects the most water and safely distributes it to the most people. This solution could help people live together more comfortably on our crowded planet.

SOLUTIONS FORM
WITHIN STEM

The world is never short on problems. Wars, famines, and climate catastrophes head a long and ever-changing list. We find solutions, but then more obstacles appear. Worldwide devastation, like that caused by the coronavirus, can change our approaches to problem-solving overnight. But if one thing is clear, it's that the most promising solutions to most of our problems depend on development of STEM methods and technologies.

When the problem is feeding the world, STEM has the only solutions. If the problem is cooling the atmosphere, STEM will show us how. If we want to avoid pandemics, STEM professionals will invent new vaccines and treatments. If we need to escape the planet, STEM researchers will learn how.

Today we hear many voices telling us to "follow the science." They are right. After all, if we follow the science, it will take us into technology, engineering, and math. Most STEM solutions are based on demonstrable facts and observations. When a solution is based on theory, its implementation is an experiment. If the experiment succeeds, the problem goes away, replaced by its solution. The solution is visible, clear, and provable. This is an example of working with "the scientific method."

This book has focused on solutions. In a way, when we tell these stories about STEM education, we are scientists describing problems, and then we examine the solutions people have tried. The most successful solutions entirely eliminate the problems. STEM provides solutions that make many of the old, intractable problems vanish.

STEM attracts young minds that welcome new information and skills. Students go on to use these skills to improve the way we all live.

When we look at it this way, STEM is the car we're driving down a brand-new expressway toward a bright future. We left the old, useless buggy at the side of a dirt road, mostly forgotten. That's behind us, and now we're ready for whatever comes our way.

SUMMARY

KEEPERS OF STEM

Throughout these pages we have noted many people and organizations who have served as keepers for the ideas of STEM education, diversity, inclusion, access, and equity.

When Black children in the southern states were being denied the benefits of STEM literacy, **Robert Moses** created a solution, one student and one class at a time. His **Algebra Project** has taught vital STEM skills to individuals all over the planet. Students entered his classroom as victims of the problem of ignorance; they left with skills, knowledge, and inspiration. Ignorance was no longer their problem. They knew enough to learn more.

LeBron James had all the usual problems of a young Black male trying to get himself a good education in the public schools of Indianapolis. One problem was transportation. He solved it by getting himself a bicycle. When he became a superstar, he knew plenty of others were still facing the same challenges. James started a school for them, emphasizing STEM skills, but he also made sure the students were given bicycles. Problem identified; problem solved.

Shirley Malcom, **Ashanti Johnson**, and **Mae Jemison** were Women of Color who faced one vexing problem after another. Often alone in their work, they confronted ignorance, apathy, and blatant racism every day. Each of them used the tools of mentorship and connection to unite colleagues and recruit more minority students into STEM programs. Some problems are gone, while others still await solutions, but these women and many others are on the case. They are the heroes of STEM and the keepers of STEM.

Those who champion diversity, inclusion, equity, and access in STEM education and training may not be risking their lives, but they are heroes. These educators, entrepreneurs, scientists, and citizens dedicate their lives to the dream of a better life for all of us. Here we will recap, noting many of these keepers and their accomplishments, and we will mention a few others.

We have described some of the contributions made by **Elon Musk** of Tesla and **Jeff Bezos** of Amazon. Today, young adventurers, like **Sinead O'Sullivan**, CEO of Northern Ireland's Fusion Space Technologies, are spearheading the next generation of innovators. These entrepreneurs have staked their careers on advances in STEM, hiring diverse teams of STEM professionals to keep their companies on the cutting edge.

Sometimes a celebrity can do a lot. We've noted **Pharrell Williams**'s **YELLOW** project and how his mother, **Dr. Carolyn Williams**, has used her expertise in education to help her son make his STEM dream come true. We've also mentioned celebrity keepers of STEM

will.i.am and **LeBron James**. The **LeBron James Family Foundation** and **i.am College Track** help hundreds of college-bound minority STEM students stay on track to become STEM heroes.

In chapter 2, we cited the influential essay on STEM diversity written by **Kenneth Gibbs Jr.** We also saw the effects of STEM diversity in the stories of businessman **Kelvin Westbrook**, television personality **Montel Williams**, and actor-doctor **Ken Jeong**. In our first account of a NASA scientist, we looked at the team efforts led by **Clayton Turner**.

Sometimes a government office can claim STEM accomplishments, and this is very true of the **Federal Deposit Insurance Corporation** (**FDIC**). Their diverse staff is skilled in math and statistics, and they back programs that encourage STEM diversity, including **Money Smart**.

In chapter 3, **Shirley Malcom** showed us the slow evolution of diversity and equity in STEM, while **Tuan Nguyen** of Kansas State University works on STEM research that shows the battle is still being fought. In this chapter, we also encountered longtime STEM education support from the **Abbott Fund** and its **Future Well Kids** program.

Chapters 3 and 4 told us about our nation's **Historically Black Colleges and Universities** (**HBCUs**) and Delaware State University's **Tony Allen**. These institutions are often where young women and minorities create a STEM future. In chapter 4, we saw further details about HBCUs and their role in STEM diversity. There, we met **Dr. Glenda Glover** and **Dr. Willis Lonzer III** and their organizations Alpha Kappa Alpha (AKA) and Alpha Phi Alpha (APA). These two people and their organizations work to encourage more diversity in STEM schooling and hiring. We also encountered STEM diversity programs sponsored by **ExxonMobil** and the **National Math &**

Science Initiative (NMSI), the US Department of Agriculture (USDA), and NASA.

Chapter 5 covered inclusion and the keepers of STEM **Sara Brownell** of **Research for Inclusive STEM Education (RISE)** and **Malesia Dunn** of the **Pittsburgh Post-Gazette (PPG) Foundation**.

Chapter 6 covered mentorship, which was so well illustrated in the stories of **Melanie Harrison Okoro**, **Ashanti Johnson**, and their program **Minorities Striving and Pursuing Higher Degrees of Success in Earth System Science (MS PHD'S)**. Mentorship was further explored in the account of **Jackie and Rachel Robinson's scholarship fund**. This chapter also covered the career of **David Northern** in our nation's public housing agencies.

In chapter 7, we saw the effects of collaboration in STEM efforts. The **New Orleans Pelicans** team up with local partners to create **STEMFEST**, which coincides with the **NBA Math Hoops program**. Not to be left behind, the **NFL Hall of Fame's Educational Outreach Program** features teachers like Houston Community College's **Jacqueline Brannon Giles**. She shows young people how their interest in sports statistics can translate into real learning about math.

Here we also saw **Ka Hei**, a STEM education project in Hawaii, and we met **Kelsey Walters**, a typically dedicated STEM teacher. And we learned about **Misti Moore**, who runs STEM education programs for **NASA**.

In chapter 8, we met **Dr. Carol O'Donnell** of the **Smithsonian Science Education Center**, who is working to create a "STEM education ecosystem."

In chapter 9, we learned about STEM proponent **William "Bill" Montgomery** and his **Hidden Pioneers** program.

These are just some of the many keepers of STEM who educate our children, train our workforce, and help our nation prepare for whatever the future might bring. Countless other organizations and individuals are involved in this effort. The benefits of STEM skills and creativity must be shared equally by all citizens.

When we include everyone and give all people access, we work better, create better, and become better people.

We help little girls and little boys everywhere, no matter the history, circumstances, or color of skin, to fly toward the light—to soar on those aerodynamic wings of STEM—toward a brighter, more inclusive future.

> *When we include everyone and give all people access, we work better, create better, and become better people.*

BIBLIOGRAPHY

AAAS. "STEM Mentoring: Emerging Strategies for Inclusion."
AAAS.org. April 4, 2019. https://www.aaas.org/sites/default/
files/2019-04/19-018%20AAAS%20STEM%20Mentoring_
final_web.pdf.

Acumen. "Patient Capital Solves Tough Problems by Bridging
Markets and Philanthropy." Acumen.org. Accessed July 13,
2022. https://acumen.org/about/patient-capital/.

AGU. "Ashanti Johnson Receives 2016 Excellence in Geophysical
Education Award." EOS.org. January 11, 2017. https://eos.
org/agu-news/ashanti-johnson-receives-2016-excellence-in-
geophysical-education-award.

Alan. "HBCUs Still Putting Blacks in STEM." *Science & Enterprise*.
July 10, 2020. https://sciencebusiness.technewslit.
com/?p=39485.

Alpha Kappa Alpha Sorority. "About AKA." AKA.
Accessed July 13, 2022. https://aka1908.com/about/.

Amazon. "Amazon Teams Up with Pharrell Williams' YELLOW and Georgia Tech to Launch New Music Remix Competition to Inspire Students to Pursue Computer Science." Amazon.com. January 19, 2021. https://press. aboutamazon.com/news-releases/news-release-details/amazon-teams-pharrell-williams-yellow-and-georgia-tech-launch.

Amazon. "STEM Club Toy Subscription: 3–4 Year Olds." Amazon.com. Accessed July 13, 2022. https://www.amazon. com/STEM-Club-Toy-Subscription-year/dp/B01M71IUZ7.

Arnim, Emily. "A Third of Minority Students Leave STEM Majors. Here's Why." EAB.com. October 8, 2019. https://eab.com/ insights/daily-briefing/student-success/a-third-of-minority-students-leave-stem-majors-heres-why/.

AWS Public Sector Blog Team. "AWS Educate Now Available to Students Ages 14 and Up." AWS. November 28, 2017. https://aws.amazon.com/blogs/publicsector/ aws-educate-now-available-to-students-ages-14-and-up/.

Berland, Evan. "GSK Announces over $1M for Local Nonprofits to Increase Equity in STEM Education and Careers; Grants Include Funding for Online Science during Pandemic." GSK. February 4, 2021. https://us.gsk.com/ en-us/media/press-releases/gsk-announces-over-1m-for-local-nonprofits-to-increase-equity-in-stem-education/#.

Bland, Leah. "Ashanti Johnson: 2016 Excellent in Earth and Space Science Education Award Winner." AGU. December 14, 2016. https://honors.agu.org/winners/ashanti-johnson-2/.

Boyer, Lauren. "From Stem Cells to STEM Diversity: Immunologist Kenneth Gibbs, Jr. Forges Equity in Science." AAAS.org. January 28, 2022. https://www.aaas.org/membership/member-spotlight/stem-cells-stem-diversity-immunologist-kenneth-gibbs-jr-forges-equity.

Boys & Girls Haven. "A Home & A Future." Boys & Girls Haven. Accessed July 13, 2022. https://boysandgirlshaven.org

BroadbandUSA. "What Is NTIA?" BroadbandUSA. Accessed July 13, 2022. https://broadbandusa.ntia.doc.gov/.

Carbonite. "About Carbonite." Carbonite.com. Accessed July 13, 2022. https://www.carbonite.com/what-is-carbonite.

Carbonite. "Carbonite Charitable Fund Reinvests in STEM Education." Carbonite.com. April 10, 2019. https://www.carbonite.com/news/article/2019/04/carbonite-charitable-fund-reinvests-in-stem-education?utm_source=twitter.com&utm_medium=social&utm_campaign=carbonite-charitable-fund-reinvests-in-stem-education.

Chatham, Luke. "New Research Center Focuses on Inclusive STEM Education." *The State Press*. September 21, 2020. https://www.statepress.com/article/2020/09/spbiztech-new-research-center-focuses-on-inclusive-stem-education.

Cotton, Karen. "PVAMU Receives $500,000 from USDA-NIFA; Funding to Create More Pathways Towards Careers in USDA, Agriculture." PVAMU.edu. May 11, 2022. https://www.pvamu.edu/blog/pvamu-receives-500000-from-usda-nifa-funding-to-create-more-pathways-towards-careers-in-usda-agriculture/.

DeAngelis, Stephen. "Celebrities and STEM Education." Enterra Solutions. October 5, 2018. https://enterrasolutions.com/blog/celebrities-and-stem-education/.

Delaware State University. "About Tony: Tony Allen Ph.D. / President." DSU. Accessed July 13, 2022. https://www.desu.edu/about/administration/president/about-tony.

Discovery Education. "Empowering a New Generation to Lead Fuller, Healthier Lives." Future Well Kids. Accessed July 13, 2020. https://futurewellkids.com.

Dodson, Christopher. "New Orleans Pelicans and Chevron Partner with Learn Fresh to Promote STEM Education." *Forbes.* July 26, 2021. https://www.forbes.com/sites/christopherdodson/2021/07/26/new-orleans-pelicans-continuing-learn-fresh-nba-math-hoops-collaboration-with-chevron/?sh=7ec4e32847c6.

Editors, The. "Role of Girl Scouts and Early Learning: Sylvia Acevedo, CEO, Girl Scouts of America." *Early Learning Nation.* January 2, 2019. https://earlylearningnation.com/2019/01/sylvia-acevedo-ceo-girl-scouts-of-the-usa/.

Education, PPG Foundation. "PPG Brings STEM Learning to PPG Paints Arena with 'Science at Play.'" PPG. Accessed July 13, 2022. https://communities.ppg.com/news/PPG-brings-STEM-learning-to-PPG-Paints-Arena-with.

Energy Factor. "Nurturing STEM Talent in the Permian Basin."
ExxonMobil. September 29, 2020. https://energyfac-
tor.exxonmobil.com/projects/community-impact/
nmsi-permian-basin/.

Engel, Jeff Bauter. "Resilient Coders Tackles Tech Diversity
Issues, One Person at a Time." Xconomy.com. November 3,
2016. https://xconomy.com/boston/2016/11/03/resilient-
coders-tackles-tech-diversity-issues-one-person-at-a-time/.

Episcopal Academy, The. "Former NFL Star John Urschel
Talks Mathematics." The Episcopal Academy.
March 31, 2021. https://www.episco-
palacademy.org/news-post-details/~post/
clare-foundation-stem-speaker-john-urschel-20210315.

ExxonMobil. "Community Engagement: STEM Education."
Corporate ExxonMobil. December 4, 2019. https://corporate.
exxonmobil.com/Sustainability/Community-engagement/
STEM-education.

FDIC. "Diversity and Inclusion." FDIC.com. January 2011.
https://www.fdic.gov/about/diversity/.

FDIC. "Resources: Money Smart." FDIC.com. April 20, 2022.
https://www.fdic.gov/resources/consumers/money-smart/
index.html.

Fregni, Jessica. "How Rural Students Are Left Behind in
the Digital Age." Teachforamerica.org. January 17, 2020.
https://www.teachforamerica.org/one-day/top-issues/
how-rural-students-are-left-behind-in-the-digital-age.

Funk, Cary, and Kim Parker. "Diversity in the STEM Workforce Varies Widely across Jobs." Pew Research Center. January 9, 2018. https://www.pewresearch.org/social-trends/2018/01/09/diversity-in-the-stem-workforce-varies-widely-across-jobs/.

Furst Group. "Does Your Board Pass the Diversity Challenge?" *Trustee.* January 22, 2016. https://www.furstgroup.com/resources/diverse-governance.

Gannon, Joyce. "PPG Commits $20 Million to Diversity and Inclusion Efforts over Next 5 Years." *Pittsburgh Post-Gazette.* July 24, 2022. https://www.post-gazette.com/business/career-workplace/2021/01/31/PPG-20-million-diversity-inclusion-equity/stories/202101310047.

Genatossio, Noah. "Roderick Raynor Paige." Blackpast.org. June 12, 2008. https://www.blackpast.org/african-american-history/paige-roderick-raynor-1933/.

Gibbs, Kenneth, Jr. "Diversity in STEM: What It Is and Why It Matters." *Scientific American.* September 10, 2014. https://blogs.scientificamerican.com/voices/diversity-in-stem-what-it-is-and-why-it-matters/.

Globus, Al. "Sourcing and Sustaining Optimum Financing." National Space Society. Accessed July 13, 2022. https://space.nss.org/settlement/nasa/spaceresvol4/newspace3.html.

Glover, Glenda. "White House Continues to Support Historically Black Colleges and Universities (HBCUs)." PRNewswire.com. October 14, 2021. https://www.prnewswire.com/news-releases/white-house-continues-to-support-historically-black-colleges-and-universities-hbcus-by-glenda-glover-phd-jd-cpa-301400651.html.

González, Juan. "From the Archives: Civil Rights Leader Bob Moses in 2010 on Fighting for Equality in Law & Education." *Democracy Now!* July 26, 2021. https://www.democracynow.org/2021/7/26/bob_moses.

Gregory, Madeleine. "How the Pandemic Is Changing STEM Education." *Sierra*. September 28, 2020. https://www.sierraclub.org/sierra/how-pandemic-changing-stem-education.

Gregory, Sara. "Pharrell Williams' Latest Project: A Private School in Norfolk for Students from Low-Income Families." *The Virginian-Pilot*. June 7, 2021. https://www.pilotonline.com/news/education/vp-nw-pharrell-williams-yellowhab-school-20210607-hhyzrj6cmjg7pae4s77tqdl3ye-story.html.

Grossman, Jennifer M., and Michelle V. Porche. "Perceived Gender and Racial/Ethnic Barriers to STEM Success." *Sage Journals* 49, no. 6 (April 22, 2013): 698–727. https://doi.org/10.1177/0042085913481364.

Hale, Laura. "Happy 60th Birthday, Interstate Highway System!" Infrastructurereportcard.org. June 29, 2016. https://infrastructurereportcard.org/happy-60th-birthday-interstate-highway-system/.

Hall, Loura. "Going to the Moon Was Hard—but the Benefits Were Huge, for All of Us." NASA. July 15, 2019. https://www.nasa.gov/directorates/spacetech/feature/Going_to_the_Moon_Was_Hard_But_the_Benefits_Were_Huge.

HBCU Today. "HBCUs with STEM Programs."
     HBCUToday.net. Accessed July 13, 2022. http://
     hbcutoday.net/index.php/hbcu-content/340-career-paths/
     hbcus-with-stem/336-hbcus-with-stem-programs.

i.am Angel Foundation. "i.am College Track."
     i.am.angelfoundation.org. Accessed July 13, 2022. https://
     www.iamangelfoundation.org/programs/i-am-college-track/.

Ibañez, Maria. "AWIS Calls on VCs, Investors to
     Expand Funding Opportunities for Women in STEM."
     AWIS. September 18, 2018. https://www.awis.org/
     venture-capitalists-investors-expand-funding-women-stem/.

Jackie Robinson Foundation. "Explore Our Roots."
     Jackierobinson.org. Accessed July 13, 2022. https://jacki-
     erobinson.org/history/.

James, LeBron. "Our Home. Our Family."
     Lebronjamesfamilyfoundation.org. Accessed July 13,
     2022. https://www.lebronjamesfamilyfoundation.
     org/i-promise-school/.

James, LeBron. "We Are Family." Ipromise.school.
     Accessed July 13, 2022. https://ipromise.school/.

Johnson, Ashanti, and Melanie Harrison Okoro. "How to Recruit
     and Retain Underrepresented Minorities." *American Scientist.*
     February 22, 2016. https://www.americanscientist.org/article/
     how-to-recruit-and-retain-underrepresented-minorities.

Jordan, David, Jr. "William Montgomery Talks about Technology,
     STEM and the 2nd Annual Global Diversity Transportation
     & Technology Summit 2022." *ESHE Magazine.* February 23,

2022. http://eshemagazine.com/2022/02/william-montgom-ery-talk-about-technology-stem-and-the-2nd-annual-global-diversity-transportation-technology-summit-2022/.

Kenney, Tanasia. "8 Black Celebrities You Didn't Know Graduated with a STEM Degree." *Atlanta Black Star.* August 29, 2016. https://atlantablackstar.com/2016/08/29/8-black-celebrities-didnt-know-graduated-stem-degree/.

Keveney, Bill. "Ken Burns: Jackie Robinson Made a 'Profound Difference.'" *USA Today.* January 18, 2016. https://www.usatoday.com/story/life/tv/2016/01/18/ken-burns-jackie-robinson-made-profound-difference/78972824/.

Killpack, Tess L., and Laverne C. Melón. "Toward Inclusive STEM Classrooms: What Personal Role Do Faculty Play?" *CBE—Life Sciences Education* 15, no. 3 (Fall 2016): es3, 1–9. https://doi.org/10.1187/cbe.16-01-0020.

Kunche, Veni. "Meet Angel D'az." Diversifytech.co. Accessed July 13, 2022. https://www.diversifytech.co/stories/angel-d-az.

Kunche, Veni. "Meet Dicko Sow." Diversifytech.co. Accessed July 13, 2022. https://www.diversifytech.co/stories/dicko-sow.

Levenson, Michael, Clay Risen, and Eduardo Medina. "Bob Moses, Crusader for Civil Rights and Math Education, Dies at 86." *New York Times.* July 25, 2021. https://www.nytimes.com/2021/07/25/us/bob-moses-dead.html.

McDonald, Samuel. "Clayton P. Turner, Director, NASA's Langley Research Center." NASA.gov. July 28, 2016. https://www.nasa.gov/feature/langley/clayton-p-turner-director-nasa-langley-research-center/.

Meyer, Beth, and Jenna Daugherty. "Paving the Way to Gender Equity through STEM Education." U.S. Chamber of Commerce Foundation. March 3, 2021. https://www.uschamberfoundation.org/blog/post/paving-way-gender-equity-through-stem-education.

Moore, Misti. "MUREP Innovation Tech Transfer Idea Competition (MITTIC)." NASA. Accessed July 13, 2022. https://www.nasa.gov/stem/murep/projects/mittic.html.

NASA. "Clayton Turner—Langley Research Center." YouTube.com. February 8, 2013. https://www.youtube.com/watch?v=e0ZyD9iVDDA.

National Park Service. "The Little Rock Nine: The End of Legal Segregation." NPS.gov. April 15, 2021. https://www.nps.gov/people/the-little-rock-nine.htm.

New England Venture Capital Association. "Hack.Diversity." Newenglandvc.org. Accessed July 13, 2022. https://newenglandvc.org/portfolio/.

Nguyen, Tuan D., and Christopher Redding. "Changes in the Demographics, Qualifications, and Turnover of American STEM Teachers, 1988–2012." *AERA Open*. July 2018. https://doi.org/10.1177/2332858418802790.

Original Sources. "Jackie Robinson, President Eisenhower, and the Little Rock Crisis." Original Sources. Accessed July 13, 2022. https://www.originalsources.com/Document. aspx?DocID=4Q1W35NJXAU3WGJ.

Peppers, Faith. "Celebrating the Agricultural Impacts of 1890 Land-Grant Universities." USDA.gov. February 23, 2021. https://www.usda.gov/media/blog/2021/02/23/ celebrating-agricultural-impacts-1890-land-grant-universities.

Pointer, Eric. "Teachers, Staff Prep for Return of Warren Township Students." FOX 59. July 28, 2021. https://fox59.com/news/ teachers-staff-prep-for-return-of-warren-township-students/.

Polin, Jane L. "A Legacy of Breaking Barriers." Candid. 2019. http://grantcraft.org/wp-content/uploads/ sites/2/2019/10/35347.pdf.

Private Equity Wire. "Women in VC Part II: Q&A with Christine Hockley, Director of Investments at British Patient Capital." Private Equity Wire. October 15, 2020. https://www.private-equitywire.co.uk/2020/10/15/290959/women-vc-part-ii-qa-christine-hockley-director-investments-british-patient.

Red Lake Nation News. "STEM NOLA Provides Critical Summer STEM Educational Programming to Louisiana Youth." Red Lake Nation News. July 1, 2021. https://www.redlakenation-news.com/story/2021/07/01/news/stem-nola-provides-critical-summer-stem-educational-programming-to-louisiana-youth/99076.html.

Reichhardt, Tony. "To the Moon by 2024: Here's the Plan." *Smithsonian Magazine*. August 2019. https://www.smithsonianmag.com/air-space-magazine/moon-rush-2024-180972600/.

Reviews.com Staff. "Bridging the Gender Divide: Guide to Overcoming Broadband Access to Be a Woman Leader in STEM." ZDNet. August 16, 2021. https://www.zdnet.com/home-and-office/networking/bridging-the-gender-divide-guide-to-overcoming-broadband-access-to-be-a-woman-leader-in-stem/.

Rollins, Marlynn. "Diversity in STEM: What Is It, Why Does It Matter, and How do We Increase It?" Sea Grant California. September 15, 2020. https://caseagrant.ucsd.edu/news/diversity-stem-what-it-why-does-it-matter-and-how-do-we-increase-it.

Route Fifty. "Broadband." Route Fifty. Accessed July 13, 2022. https://www.route-fifty.com/topic/broadband/.

Shetterly, Margot Lee. "Hidden Figures." Hiddenfigures.com. 2016. http://www.hiddenfigures.com/cast-and-crew.

Smart, Ashley. "After Years of Gains, Black STEM Representation Is Falling. Why?" Undark.com. September 11, 2020. https://undark.org/2020/09/11/after-years-of-gains-black-stem-representation-is-falling-why/.

Smith, Tara. "Collaboration: At the Root of STEM Success." Tech & Learning. October 26, 2016. https://www.techlearning.com/resources/collaboration-at-the-root-of-stem-success.

Smithsonian Institute. "Carol O'Donnell: Director, Smithsonian Science Education Center." Smithsonian Institute. 2021. https://www.si.edu/about/bios/carol-odonnell.

STATtrak. "The Struggles and Wonders of a First-Generation STEM Student." Stattrak.org. October 1, 2017. https://stattrak.amstat.org/2017/10/01/stem_struggle/.

Steverson, Bryan. "Jackie Robinson's Life Showed the Power of Role Models." Knox News. April 23, 2016. https://archive.knoxnews.com/opinion/columnists/jackie-robinsons-life-showed-the-power-of-role-models-30c4a115-e841-58a6-e053-0100007f9ba2-376788001.html/.

Steverson, Bryan. "Journey to Justice: The Converging Paths of Jackie Robinson and Dr. Martin Luther King Jr." Society for American Baseball Research. Accessed July 13, 2022. https://sabr.org/journal/article/journey-to-justice-the-converging-paths-of-jackie-robinson-and-dr-martin-luther-king-jr/.

TAAHP. "David A. Northern Sr. to Take Helm at Houston Housing Authority." TAAHP.org. February 9, 2022. https://taahp.org/david-a-northern-sr-to-take-helm-at-houston-housing-authority/.

Tabeling, Katie. "Biden Taps DSU President Allen to Head HBCU Board." Delaware Business Times. September 8, 2021. https://delawarebusinesstimes.com/news/biden-taps-allen-hbcu-board/.

Trumbore, Dave. "Secret Science Nerds: Ken Jeong
        Doesn't Just Play a Doctor on TV." Nerdist.com. December
        16, 2016. https://archive.nerdist.com/secret-science-nerds-
        ken-jeong-doesnt-just-play-a-doctor-on-tv/.

University of Massachusetts Amherst. "Study Finds New Mentoring
        Model Supports Underrepresented Minority Women Faculty
        in STEM." Phys.org. June 22, 2020. https://phys.org/
        news/2020-06-underrepresented-minority-women-faculty-
        stem.html.

US Department of Education. "Number and Percentage
        Distribution of Science, Technology, Engineering, and Math-
        ematics (STEM) Degrees/Certificates Conferred by Post-
        secondary Institutions, by Race/Ethnicity, Level of Degree/
        Certificate, and Sex of Student: 2009-10 through 2018-19."
        National Center for Education Statistics. Table 318.45.
        Accessed July 13, 2022. https://nces.ed.gov/programs/digest/
        d20/tables/dt20_318.45.asp.

US Department of Education. "Rod Paige, U.S. Secretary of
        Education—Biography." USDE. August 23, 2003. https://
        www2.ed.gov/news/staff/bios/paige-kids.html.

UTEP News Archive. "UTEP Secures $500K STEM Grant from
        NASA." UTEP. Accessed July 13, 2022. http://news.utep.edu/
        nasa-stem-education-grant/.

Voorhees College. "Voorhees College Prepares for
        In-Person MLK Celebration Program." Voorhees College.
        January 7, 2022. https://www.voorhees.edu/news/voorhees-
        college-prepares-for-in-person-mlk-celebration-program.

Wells, Honor Warren. "Fantastic NFL Data in
Culturally Diverse Classrooms." Bleacher Report. April 10,
2009. https://bleacherreport.com/articles/154039-fantastic-
nfl-data-in-culturally-diverse-classrooms.

Whitaker, Justin. "State Awards IU $4.4 Million to Help Recover
Lost Learning for K-12 Schools." Indiana University. July 20,
2021. https://news.iu.edu/stories/2021/07/iu/releases/20-
student-learning-recovery-grants.html.

Whitcomb, Remington. "Carlotta Walls LaNier of the Little
Rock Nine Gives Interview at Robert H. Jackson Center." *The
Post-Journal*. May 23, 2017. https://www.post-journal.com/
news/page-one/2017/05/carlotta-walls-lanier-of-the-little-
rock-nine-gives-interview-at-robert-h-jackson-center/.

White House, The. "President Biden Announces Intent to Appoint
Dr. Tony Allen as Chair of the President's Board of Advisors
on Historically Black Colleges and Universities." White-
house.gov. September 8, 2021. https://www.whitehouse.gov/
briefing-room/statements-releases/2021/09/08/president-
biden-announces-intent-to-appoint-dr-tony-allen-as-chair-
of-the-presidents-board-of-advisors-on-historically-black-
colleges-and-universities/.

Wikimedia Foundation. "Melanie Harrison Okoro." Wikipedia.
Last modified June 15, 2022. https://en.wikipedia.org/wiki/
Melanie_Harrison_Okoro.

Wikimedia Foundation. "Patient Capital." Wikipedia.

Last modified December 21, 2021. https://en.wikipedia.org/
wiki/Patient_capital.

Wikimedia Foundation. "Shirley M. Malcom." Wikipedia.
Last modified March 31, 2022. https://en.wikipedia.org/wiki/
Shirley_M._Malcom.

Wilson, Jonathan. "Baltimore SEMAA at Morgan State University."
Morgan State University. Accessed July 13, 2022. https://
www.morgan.edu/semaa.

Wilson, Lucy. "Understanding Patient Capital & Why It's
Important for Startups." Beauhurst.com. November 18, 2021.
https://www.beauhurst.com/blog/patient-capital/.

Yates, Shanique. "Meet Dr. Ashanti Johnson, the First Black
Woman to Be a Chemical Oceanographer in the U.S."
Afrotech. March 19, 2021. https://afrotech.com/meet-dr-
ashanti-johnson-the-first-black-woman-to-be-a-chemical-
oceanographer-in-the-u-s.

YELLOW. "Change Starts at Home—the Heart
of YELLOW Is Virginia Beach." Teamyellow.org.
September 8, 2020. https://teamyellow.org/stories/
change-starts-at-home-the-heart-of-yellow-is-virginia-beach.

YELLOW. "Entrepreneur Advice from Kamryn,
Fifth-Grader and Entrepreneur." Teamyellow.org. June 23,
2021. https://teamyellow.org/stories/entrepreneurial-advice-
from-kamryn-fifth-grader-and-entrepreneur.